MOTHER JONES

MOTHER JONES

Kathlyn Gay

MORGAN REYNOLDS
PUBLISHING
Greensboro, North Carolina

american workers

The Homestead Steel Strike of 1892

The Pullman Strike of 1894

The Ludlow Massacre of 1913-14

Mother Jones

MOTHER JONES

Library of Congress Cataloging-in-Publication Data

Gay, Kathlyn.
  Mother Jones / Kathlyn Gay.
       p. cm.
  Includes bibliographical references and index.
  ISBN-13: 978-1-59935-016-5 (library binding)
  ISBN-10: 1-59935-016-5 (library binding)
   1. Jones, Mother, 1843?-1930—Juvenile literature. 2. Labor
leaders—United States—Biography—Juvenile literature. 3. Labor
unions—Organizing—Great Britain—History—Juvenile literature. 4.
Women in the labor movement—United States—Biography—
Juvenile literature. I. Title.
  HD8073.J6G39 2006
  331.88092—dc22

                          2005034713

Printed in the United States of America
First Edition

CONTENTS

Mother Jones. (Library of Congress)

1.
Born to Agitate

On September 6, 1912, a small woman—barely five feet tall—took her place on a makeshift platform in the public square by the courthouse in Charleston, West Virginia. Mary Jones examined her audience through her wire-rimmed glasses. She wore a long black dress with lace at the neck. Her black hat covered her white hair except for a neat bun at the back of her head. She appeared to be someone's grandmother. But her words soon belied that image. She began in a low voice, and the audience, a crowd of striking miners, hushed to listen intently. All could hear Mary Jones's indignation, her quiet fury as she spoke:

This great gathering that is here tonight signals there is a disease in the State that must be wiped out.

The people have suffered from that disease patiently; they have borne insults, oppression, outrages; they appealed to their chief executive, they appealed to the courts, they appealed to the attorney general, and in every case they were turned down. They were ignored.

The disease Mary Jones was referring to was coal-mining-company owners and government officials who did nothing to better the deplorable working conditions in mines. Men and young boys worked long hours underground for meager pay. Most miners' families lived in miserable poverty, and Jones often visited the families to give them whatever money, food, and clothing she could spare. Because of her concern, miners called her "Mother Jones."

A West Virginia coal miner's shack. Mother Jones devoted much of her life's work to making public the social injustice that afflicted the working class. (Library of Congress)

For most of her adult life, Mary Harris Jones agitated and organized on behalf of industrial workers. Although she dressed conservatively, she acted unconventionally. She often addressed workers using fiery language, sometimes saying she was there to raise hell. She scolded, cajoled, and demanded that laborers work together through unions for their own and their fellow workers' welfare. Today, it would not be unusual for a woman to be a labor organizer, but this was a dangerous job for anyone, particularly a woman, during the industrial revolution of the late 1800s and early 1900s. As Mary Jones points out in her autobiography, the late nineteenth and early twentieth centuries were a tumultuous time for labor: "In all the great industrial centers the working class was in rebellion. . . . Throughout the country, there was business depression and much unemployment. In the cities, there was hunger and rags and despair."

In mining country, there were not only rebellions but also brutal conflicts between miners and mining company officials, whether in West Virginia, Pennsylvania, southern Illinois, Colorado, or elsewhere. Jones not only spoke to miners but also to factory, textile, railroad, and steel workers, and laborers of all types across the United States. Mary Harris "Mother" Jones was an outspoken activist on behalf of the poor and one of the most inspiring labor leaders in U.S. history. What made her unusual was not just her gender but the fact that she came to organizing so late in life and that she gave herself so entirely to the cause.

Jones's hometown of Cork, located on Ireland's southern coast. (King George III Topographical Collection)

At the beginning of her autobiography, Jones declares, "I was born in the city of Cork, Ireland, in 1830." But some historians contend that this is not the actual date of Mary's birth. Rather it is a date she picked later in her life in order to exaggerate her role as an elderly firebrand. Historical documents, including court records and school certificates, vary and indicate Mary was born in 1836 or 1837, or perhaps as late as 1843. According to one source, her parents, Richard and Helen Cotter Harris, had Mary baptized on August 1, 1837, at St. Mary's Cathedral in Cork. Since the Harrises were Catholics, they followed the church practice of infant baptism. Thus, the date suggests Mary was born years later than her autobiography claims. Her baptism date also contradicts Mary's assertion that her birthday was May 1. In fact, she proclaimed she was born on May 1 only after that day became known as the international workers' holiday, first celebrated in 1886. By that time, she was closely associated with labor's cause.

In spite of confusion regarding her early years, there is no doubt that Mary Harris grew up in an atmosphere of protest and political turmoil. Her father was a tenant farmer who struggled to provide for his wife and five children. Like other poor farmers, Richard Harris rented a small plot of land in the village of Inchigeelagh (pronounced Inch-ee-*gee*-lah, with a hard g as in girl), where he grew a few vegetable crops, primarily potatoes.

Tenant farmers paid their rent with the crops they grew and sold. The British owned most of the Irish farmland, and many landowners, the so-called gentry, were Protestants living in England. Under British rule, Irish Catholics were not allowed to buy land and could not enter a profession.

When Richard Harris could no longer support his family in the rural village, he moved them to the seaport town of Cork, where Mary's younger sib-lings—Catherine (1840), Ellen (1845), and William (1846)—were born. They lived in a crowded section of the city, where many other poor Irish families settled. But Harris managed to keep his Inchigeelagh land to grow food, and the family went back and forth from town to the countryside as the seasons dictated.

According to some historians, Mary believed her father and grandfather were involved in numerous efforts, some of them violent, to change the living conditions of poor peasants and to gain Irish freedom from British rule. Some accounts say that the army arrested her grandfather because of his rebellious acts, and hanged him. At the time, secret societies were common in rural areas, and those who were members of rebel groups, known by such names as the Molly Maguires and Rockites, used violent tactics to strike out against injustice. They might seek revenge for high rents or home evictions, for example, by beating up a wealthy farmer or killing his livestock. Some stories about the Harris family suggest that authorities labeled Richard Harris a menace. The army claimed that Mary's father was a conspirator—one of the secret society of men who burned landowners' homes, barns, and crops. He is said to have sailed for North America to escape.

Another scenario suggests that Richard Harris and his eldest son, Richard Jr., were among millions of Irish who fled their homeland during the mid-1800s because of a potato famine. Potatoes were the staple food in Ireland, and loss of the crop created great devastation that was exacerbated when landowners evicted masses of Irish peasants from their pitiable mud homes because they could not pay rent. Many evicted families crowded into workhouses, which bred disease and resulted in more deaths. The *Cork Examiner,* a weekly county newspaper, reported deaths every week from starvation:

> Disease and death in every quarter—the once hardy
> population worn away to emaciated skeletons—
> fever, dropsy, diarrhea, and famine rioting in every
> filthy hovel, and sweeping away whole families . . .
> 400 men starving in one district, having no
> employment . . . a whole village in the last stage of
> destitution . . . dead bodies of children flung into
> holes hastily scratched in the earth, without a shroud
> or coffin . . . every field becoming a grave, and the
> land a wilderness.

Many peasants hoped to escape disease, starvation, and death by emigrating. Hundreds of thousands of Irish sought homes in Great Britain, Canada, and the United States. They made the ocean crossing in the cargo area of flimsy ships that became known as "coffin ships" because so many died on the way. Many of these ships to Canada were detained on the border at Grosse Isle. Passengers were placed in quarantine sheds, where countless numbers died. One account described the horrors on a ship that sailed from Cork as:

> crowded beyond its utmost capacity of stowage
> with unhappy beings of all ages, with fever raging
> in their midst . . . miserable passengers unable to
> help themselves, or afford the least relief to each
> other; one-fourth, or one-third, or one-half of the
> entire number in different stages of the disease;
> many dying, some dead; the fatal poison intensified

Hundreds of Irish immigrants crowd on board a "coffin ship" bound for America. The typical journey took the passengers from Cork to Liverpool, England, and then on to the United States and Canada. (Courtesy of the Granger Collection.)

by the indescribable foulness of the air breathed . . . the wails of the children, the ravings of the delirious, the cries and groans of those in mortal agony!

Mary's father and brother were fortunate to survive their trip to North America and find a place to live in a Burlington, Vermont, boarding house not far from the Canadian border. Like many other immigrants, father and son found jobs as laborers with a railroad construction crew, and Richard Harris became a naturalized U.S. citizen. By the time the Harrises had earned enough money to pay for their family's passage across the

Atlantic, they were working with the railroad crew in Canada; the Harris family reunited in Toronto, Ontario, just over the border from the United States.

Young Mary hoped to be a teacher, one of the few jobs outside the home open to women. She grew up in Toronto and attended public school there, "but always as the child of an American citizen," she wrote. "Of that citizenship I have ever been proud." She did well in her studies and years later told a reporter that she received "a good brand of popular education" and also learned "some things which they probably did not have in mind. Among the details of my education was a hatred of injustice and a vast inquisitiveness." This motivated her to see for herself "the truth about conditions" for industrial workers.

Founded in 1847, the Toronto Normal School enrolled future schoolmasters and schoolmistresses to serve the growing need for formally trained educators. (National Archives of Canada)

As a teenager, Mary Harris enrolled in Normal School, a teacher-training institution in Toronto. She studied for less than a year, then decided to strike out on her own. She left Canada and moved across the border to take a teaching job at a convent in Monroe, Michigan. Convent records say, "Miss M. Harris entered the house as a secular teacher on August 31, 1859." She stayed for six months and was "paid in full . . . $36.43."

Moving south of the border marked the beginning of Mary's exposure to the growing industrialization in the United States—the factories, mills, and mines that employed millions of unskilled workers, most of them immigrants. She would become caught up in the lives of these workers, people without power and subject to the whims of the wealthy ruling class.

2.

Marriage, Children, and Tragedy

Once Mary Harris left Canada, she had little contact with her family. If she was ever lonely or homesick, there is no hint of that in her writings or in any of the hundreds of speeches she gave. In fact, she offers only brief statements in her autobiography about her early adult life, and just a few sentences describe her teaching experiences.

Mary Harris was a natural teacher, however, and was constantly teaching others throughout her adult years. She claimed she disliked the profession, but what she truly disliked was "bossing little children." Instead, she said she preferred sewing, having become a proficient seamstress while in Normal School. So she decided to try her hand at dressmaking, traveling to Chicago to work in a small shop.

By the second half of the nineteenth century, Memphis was a fast-growing city with an active port along the Mississippi River that attracted both laborers and investors. (Library of Congress)

No record indicates whether Mary Harris had an independent business or worked as a seamstress for one of the many shops owned by textile manufacturers. Immigrant women, including many from Ireland and Canada, often found jobs at low wages in company-owned shops sewing precut material into finished clothing. Some did the same kind of work in their homes.

Harris soon tired of sewing dresses, and in 1860, she moved once again—this time to Memphis, Tennessee. Founded in 1819 as a community of about fifty people, Memphis sits on a bluff overlooking the Mississippi

River. Initially settled by Irish and German immigrants, Memphis soon became a shipping and industrial center, with goods transported in and out on river barges and by rail. A shipyard also added to the flourishing economy of the city.

After Harris found a job as a teacher in Memphis, she met George Jones, a blacksmith and member of the Iron Molders' Union. The couple married in 1861, the year the Civil War erupted, and eventually had four children: Catherine, Elizabeth, Terence, and Mary. Mary stayed home with the children while George worked at the Union Iron Works. They lived in a neighborhood where other workers had settled, one part of which was called Pinchgut. It was named for the famished look of the poor people who lived there; many were underfed Irish railroad workers.

Tennessee was part of the Confederacy during the Civil War. Most of the battles were fought east and south of Memphis, which was a supply depot for the Confederates until Union General Ulysses S. Grant realized he and his army could be victorious if they controlled the depots and forts along the riverways, including Memphis. In early June 1862, at least 10,000 Memphis residents watched from the bluffs as Union soldiers captured the Memphis harbor and railroad stations, thus cutting off Confederate supplies.

In spite of the bloody war between the North and South, the Jones family seemed barely touched by the strife. But they were affected by "the other civil war," as one historian called it—the ongoing struggle between the wealthy industrialists reaping huge profits from the war and the workers who labored for them. By 1864, about 200,000 male and female workers nationwide were members of trade unions. Shoemakers, railroad employees, carpenters, painters, printers, sugar packers, glass cutters, stage drivers, gun makers, and many other tradespeople went on strike to press their demands for higher wages. Workers complained bitterly that they could not afford the increased prices for food and other goods because of the war. All across the country during the Civil War, workers walked off their jobs, and in some cases, the Union Army had to send in troops to break up strikes.

The ongoing war created a labor shortage, so President Abraham Lincoln asked Congress to pass legislation that would allow employers to import immigrant labor. The Contract Labor Law of 1864 stated that foreign workers could be asked to sign a contract promising to give up as much as a year's wages to their new employer in return for having their travel expenses paid. This new source of cheap labor was often used to break strikes—at least until the law was repealed after the Civil War.

The end of the Civil War saw many former soldiers returning home and looking for work. Increased industrialization meant most of the jobs available were in large factories, which facilitated the development of unions. As new unions formed and memberships increased, so did strikes and other agitation. Mary Jones no doubt heard about the labor unrest from her husband, and she also read about union goals in the *Iron Molders' International Journal* that came to their home every month. In addition, she went along with her husband when he recruited ironworkers to join the union. But her main job was caring for their children, cooking and cleaning for the family, and using her sewing skills to make and mend their clothing.

Life for the Jones family was fairly comfortable, although in their overcrowded neighborhood sanitation was poor. A nearby swampland was like an open sewer and bred disease, which was evident when a terrible yellow-fever epidemic swept through Memphis in 1867, killing an estimated 2,500 people. The Jones's neighborhood was hit especially hard.

Yellow-fever epidemics had hit Memphis before, and outbreaks of cholera, smallpox, and dysentery were also common. Little, if any, medical treatment was available. At the time, no one knew that mosquitoes transmitted the virus that caused yellow fever. Those infected suffered fevers, chills, and severe pains. They vomited blood and stomach acids, a black mix that was a sure sign of the disease. In some cases, the skin became jaundiced, turning yellow, which is why the disease became known as yellow fever. Epidemics ceased only when the first frost came and killed the mosquitoes.

When the epidemic struck Memphis during the summer of 1867, churches closed and officials banned public gatherings. If a family member became ill, his or

The yellow-fever epidemics of the mid-1800s caused tragedy and upheaval across the country. In this illustration from Harper's Weekly, *a mob of angry citizens storms the Quarantine Marine Hospital in New York to free the patients and burn what they considered to be an unsanitary facility.* (Library of Congress)

her house was quarantined—no one could visit. Most of the wealthy citizens left town, escaping to places where the disease was not prevalent. But people without the means to flee could only stay amidst the reek of burning sulfur, which was thought to ward off disease, and the sound of creaking wagons that rolled through the streets to pick up the dead.

The Jones family was among those who had no choice but to suffer through the epidemic. No words better describe the situation than those of Mary Jones herself:

> Across the street from me, ten persons lay dead
> from the plague. The dead surrounded us. They
> were buried at night quickly and without ceremony.
> All about my house I could hear weeping and the
> cries of delirium. One by one, my four little children
> sickened and died. I washed their little bodies and
> got them ready for burial. My husband caught the
> fever and died. I sat alone through nights of grief.
> No one came to me. No one could. Other homes
> were as stricken as was mine. All day long, all night
> long, I heard the grating of the wheels of the death
> cart.

Though her autobiography is often extremely partisan, there is nothing biased about her grief. Within a short period, Mary Harris Jones's family was gone. She was left destitute, although she received some financial help from the Iron Molders, and the union honored George Jones with a funeral.

Mary Jones could easily have given in to her grief and despair, but that was not her nature. She was a fighter. She received a permit from the city to nurse the sick, going from house to house to offer whatever assistance she could. Her actions symbolized a slogan that she used later on in one form or another: "Pray for the dead and fight like hell for the living!" When the yellow-fever epidemic ended in December, Jones left Memphis, and headed back to Chicago, where she hoped to start anew.

In downtown Chicago, Jones and a partner opened a

dressmaking shop that catered to wealthy clients. Many of the clients lived in luxury buildings along Lake Michigan. While sewing for the elite, Jones often contrasted the lives of these "aristocrats," as she called them, with "the poor, shivering wretches, jobless and hungry, walking along the frozen lake front. My employers seemed neither to notice nor to care."

Chicago was not the only city where employers were oblivious to the jobless and hungry. Wherever they were located, the owners of big businesses—railroads, oil, steel, banking—were making huge profits with little thought about worker health or protections. To corporations, workers were like machinery that could be replaced. The period from about the 1870s to 1900 came to be known as the Gilded Age, named after Mark Twain's book of the same title in which he derided the corruption of the federal government and big business. Those in power believed that the production and distribution of goods should be privately owned and managed, and that government should stay out of business activities. Government at all levels became corrupt, as those in power took bribes to pass legislation that favored business and left workers unprotected. Laborers had no legal recourse when unsafe working conditions led to poor health, injuries, or death.

As industries expanded, business tycoons such as Andrew Carnegie (steel), J. P. Morgan (banking), Jay Gould (railroads), and John D. Rockefeller (oil) amassed great wealth. They were called robber barons because

The caption of this nineteenth-century political cartoon reads, "History Repeats Itself: The Robber Barons of the Middle Ages and the Robber Barons of To-day." (Courtesy of the Granger Collection.)

they got rich through ruthless business deals. With their huge corporations they created monopolies, cut off competition, and kept prices high and wages low.

An economic depression that began in 1873 added to the misery of the poor and created vast numbers of unemployed. Veterans of the Civil War, along with countless immigrants, were looking for work. In the cities, people lived in tenements and cellars of buildings that were death traps—fire hazards full of vermin and disease.

Tenements were some of the first buildings to be devoured by the great Chicago Fire in 1871, collapsing so fast that some observers of the time compared the

Residents stream across the Randolph Street Bridge on Chicago's waterfront as the fire rips through the city's downtown during the Chicago Fire of 1871. (Library of Congress)

sound to an earthquake. The cause of the historic fire is unknown, but legend says that a cow owned by Patrick and Catherine O'Leary kicked over a lantern, igniting the barn in which it was kept. The O'Leary family lived west of downtown, and once the flames burned the barn, the fire spread rapidly because of recent dry weather.

The great fire burned Chicago's central business district to the ground, consuming wooden buildings—homes, mansions, churches, businesses—including Mary Jones's downtown dressmaking shop. She lost all of her belongings and was among the 100,000 people left homeless by the fire.

Like others fleeing the flames and smoke, Jones rushed to the lakeshore, occasionally going into the water to cool off. Some who fled burning buildings close to Lake Michigan had to submerge themselves in the lake in order to save themselves from fire. The wooden streets, sidewalks, and bridges burned, and even the grease on the Chicago River ignited in places.

After a night and day without food, Jones was able to find shelter at Old St. Mary's Church on Wabash Avenue, where she stayed with other refugees until she could find a place to go. She received a sewing machine as a gift from the city and was soon able to support herself again with her dressmaking skills.

But her life was about to change dramatically. Near the church, she came across a meeting place for a group called the Knights of Labor.

3.

Becoming an Activist

While Jones temporarily lived in St. Mary's Church, she spent her evenings walking around the ruins of the neighborhood, where she found an old building, blackened by the fire but still intact. She learned that members of the Noble and Holy Order of the Knights of Labor met in the building. The Knights had originated in 1869 in Philadelphia as a secret society of tailors. Secrecy was necessary, the organization believed, to protect its members from retaliation by their employers.

The Knights hoped to bring together both skilled and unskilled workers, male and female, to form one big union. They also campaigned for the eight-hour workday and opposed child labor. To pressure employers, the Knights advocated boycotting a company—refusing to buy its goods—rather than going on strike, although radical Knights sometimes organized strikes anyway.

The Knights held meetings where speakers described their goal of helping workers to share in the wealth they created. Jones began to attend evening meetings and on Sundays went out to the woods where the Knights gathered. She listened to "splendid speakers" and liked what she heard. Some of the speakers talked about the historical ties between Socialist ideas and labor organizations in Europe.

Socialists reject capitalism and believe that the means of producing goods and services should be owned by the government and managed through collectives controlled by workers. In a Socialist system, people would work cooperatively, and workers would have the political power and means to produce and distribute goods. As the Knights spelled out their Socialist ideas, Jones soon became a supporter of their cause, although women were not admitted as members of the Knights until 1881. She also became "more and more engrossed in the labor struggle." As she explained, "I decided to take an active part in the efforts of the working people to better the conditions under which they worked and lived."

Being active meant that Jones went through Chicago neighborhoods, voluntarily spreading the word about the Knights and recruiting members for the union. She continued her work as a seamstress and kept whatever money she earned in cash because of her distrust of banks and most other institutions. She also was suspicious of people in official positions—even those in unions. In the opinion of one labor organizer, she was at her best out in the field rather than in a union office, where "she was out of place quarreling with officials, offering no constructive policy of her own and constantly violating union policy." But the organizer noted that Jones had a talent for oratory: "With one speech she often threw a whole community on strike, and she could keep the strikers loyal month after month on empty stomachs and behind bars."

Jones became a familiar face to workers and the poor, and people often gathered to hear her speak. In Chicago, as well as in other urban areas across the United States, the signs of poverty were evident in many neighborhoods. With trade union backing, thousands of the jobless gathered for huge public meetings and demonstrations. In Chicago, unemployed marchers demanded that the city provide "bread for the needy, clothing for the naked, and houses for the homeless." There were no government programs set up to care for people who had no food or shelter, but the city did respond with aid for thousands of families, though not nearly enough to help all those in need.

As Jones began to gain nationwide recognition for her speaking and organizing skills, workers called on her to help them organize strikes. In her autobiography, she wrote that she was asked to help out in the Great Railroad Strike of 1877, the first general nationwide strike in the United States. Some historians have debunked Jones's claim that workers sent for her and that she "knew the strikers personally." Whether Jones was involved or not, she certainly would have known about the general strike, prompted in part by the ongoing economic depression, which had begun in 1873. Working-class people—union and nonunion—were suffering. By 1877, three million people were unemployed. When the jobless could not pay their rent, landlords evicted them from their homes. Homeless and hungry people were ready to rebel against the big corporations, and railroads were a prime target.

Four major railroad companies cut wages even though the companies continued to earn profits and pay dividends to their stockholders. In July, railroad brakemen and firemen in Martinsburg, West Virginia, walked off their jobs and uncoupled train engines, running them into the roundhouse. They prevented hundreds of freight trains from moving goods.

Strikes quickly spread north, south, and west to cities such as Pittsburgh, Chicago, St. Louis, and San Francisco. Steel workers, miners, and other laborers joined the strike. Farmers, who hated the railroads because of the high fees charged for transporting their products, supported strikers by giving them food. Riots broke out in some cities as strike supporters, many of them nonunion people, burned railcars, tore up tracks, and destroyed railroad bridges.

In Reading, Pennsylvania, railroad workers and coal miners joined forces to strike. During one July evening,

During the great railroad strike of 1877, workers across the country organized to coordinate their efforts. This contemporary newspaper drawing shows Robert M. Ammon, leader of the strike effort in Pittsburgh and Fort Wayne, directing the movements of the strikers. (Library of Congress)

people there gathered to see a train that had been stopped on a section of track that went through the city. The militia arrived, and Joseph A. Dacus, editor of the *St. Louis Republican,* witnessed what happened when troops advanced on the crowd:

> Steadily they approached, when suddenly three hundred rifles were discharged in volleys, and five men dropped to the pavements. . . . Quite a number of revolver shots were returned by parties in the crowd. The troops continued their firing, and men, women, and children fled in fear. . . . In five minutes the streets were cleared, stores were closed, and hotels and restaurants were locked up. . . . The

streets resembled a small battle field, and the pavements were stained with many pools of blood.

In Illinois, railroad workers, laborers from steel mills, packing houses, and factories, and even crews from ships on Lake Michigan shut down railroad yards in Chicago, the rail center of the United States. Vigilantes, the National Guard, and federal troops attempted to restore order, but there were bloody encounters between mobs and police, prompting the *Chicago Times* to warn in a headline: TERRORS REIGN, THE STREETS OF CHICAGO GIVEN OVER TO HOWLING MOBS OF THIEVES AND CUTTHROATS. Actions to halt rail traffic spread to other Illinois towns. In the southern part of the state, coal miners stopped working in support of the strike.

Years later, Jones testified before Congress that "the feeling at that time of many workers and sympathizers was one of distrust, and in many instances amounted to hatred, because the corporations . . . were open and successful in passing anti-labor legislation." She explained that an "outraged populace" set fire to train locomotives in Pittsburgh. The destruction, she testified, was not the fault of railroad workers and strikers. "I know most of the strikers; all had done everything they could to keep order," she said.

The general railroad strike ended after a few weeks. Railroads agreed to restore some wage cuts, but they also hired more company police to put down union activity. The great strike raised public awareness about workers' needs, and workers discovered that only with a strong organization would it be possible to fight the power of big business supported by government.

Labor unrest continued into the 1880s, with workers of all kinds taking to the streets, striking and rioting. This led to a crackdown by police. Even when workers met peacefully to discuss wages and working hours, police broke up the gatherings. The police were urged on by employers and newspaper editors who detested unions. In Jones's words, "The workers asked only for bread and a shortening of the long hours of toil. . . . The police gave them clubs."

Poor wages and terrible working conditions in numerous industries led to strike after strike across the United States. Strikes were so frequent during the 1880s that the period became known as the "great upheaval." In one year alone, 1886, a total of 610,00 workers went on strike.

The decade also saw an appalling persecution of a particular group of workers: the Chinese. Companies brought Chinese workers to the United States to construct railroads, work in mines, and do other back-breaking labor. Many white laborers resented the Chinese because they were willing to work long hours for low wages. On the West Coast, people feared that large numbers of Chinese and other Asians would come into the country and compete for jobs. The Workingmen's Party of California conducted political campaigns to oust the Chinese.

Chinese laborers played an essential role in the building of the Transcontinental Railroad. In this 1877 photograph, Chinese workers in the Sierra Nevada fill in a valley with dirt from the mountainside. This arduous work was performed to avoid fixing the hazardous and hastily constructed trestle that orginally spanned the valley. (Library of Congress)

Jones was among those who supported the exclusion. Years later, she explained that organized mine workers "made the government in Washington put a stop to the Chinese coming in to invade the American labor movement. . . . I had a hand in that agitation; we kept it up and stopped the Chinese coming over." Such sentiment was so widespread that in 1882, Congress passed the Chinese Exclusion Act, which prohibited Chinese immigration for ten years and banned citizenship for Chinese immigrants already in the United States. (The law was renewed and extended until 1943.)

THE ULTIMATE CAUSE.

"But why is it," asked the thoughtful Chinese, "that I may go to your heaven, while I may not go to your country?"

The American missionary shrugged his shoulders. "There is no Labor vote in heaven!" said he.

A contemporary magazine cover critiques the popular sentiment in support of the exclusion of Chinese labor. (Library of Congress)

Jones's racist views were somewhat inconsistent, since she agitated for and admired African-American workers, and organized countless numbers of immigrant workers from European countries. She also supported anarchist workers—foreign- and American-born—who were feared by the majority of U.S. citizens.

Anarchism is a political theory that opposes power structures in any form. Anarchists want to create a society within which people cooperate as equals. In the United States, anarchists agitated against capitalism and were adamantly opposed to what they called wage slavery—low wages for long hours. In cities such as Chicago, Milwaukee, and New York, anarchists spoke out in support of an eight-hour workday.

Chicago became the major center for anarchist ideas, and five anarchist newspapers published in the city spread their views. When anarchists held rallies in Chicago, Jones often attended to listen to what the orators had to say. However, she wrote, "I never endorsed the philosophy of anarchism." Jones was also critical of some of the anarchists' tactics, especially when they organized a parade of poverty-stricken people in the 1880s. The parade route was along Prairie Avenue, where many wealthy employers lived. Carrying the anarchist black flag, the marchers were "in rags and tatters, in thin clothes, in wretched shoes." In Jones's view the parade was "an insane move on the part of the anarchists, as it only served to make feeling more bitter. As a matter of fact, it had no educational value whatever and only served to increase the employers' fear, to make the police more savage, and the public less sympathetic to the real distress of the workers." The general public in Chicago was unsympathetic to the workers, and their ire was further stirred in 1886 following incidents at the McCormick Harvester Machine Company outside the city.

Cyrus McCormick was determined to rid his company of unions, and workers had been striking intermittently for years. That February, workers walked out again and stayed out for several months. The company hired nonunion workers, often referred to derisively as scabs, to replace strikers. On May 3, striking workers held a mass meeting about a block from the McCormick plant. When the scabs left the factory, they clashed with strikers, and the police were called. They clubbed and shot strikers, killing several of them.

The next day, labor leaders led a protest meeting at Haymarket Square in Chicago, a grimy area of tenements, rail lines, and saloons. Because the crowd was not as large as expected, the meeting was moved to a nearby alleyway, and speakers used a wagon as a platform. Although the gathering was peaceful, police arrived and demanded that everyone disperse. Seconds later, a bomb was thrown at police from a window of a building near the square. One policeman was killed and dozens were injured. Six other policemen later died of their injuries. Police immediately began firing on the crowd, wounding more than one hundred people and killing several.

Frank Leslie's illustrated newspaper portrayed the Haymarket affair as riotous and apocalyptic in this engraving from May 15, 1886. (Library of Congress)

"The city went insane and the newspapers did everything to keep it like a madhouse. The workers' cry for justice was drowned in the shriek for revenge," Jones reported. Police believed anarchists were responsible for the killings and, without search warrants, ransacked homes, offices, meeting halls, and other places that anarchists gathered. Thirty-one people were indicted for the bombing and for conspiring to commit murder. Eight men eventually stood trial on the charges.

There was no proof that the Haymarket Eight, as they were called, had any stake in the police deaths. But the judge, jury, and state attorney made no secret of their bias against the defendants. The state attorney told the jury to "convict these men, make examples of them, hang them and you save our institutions and our society."

All the men were convicted, and seven were sentenced to death by hanging; the eighth received a fifteen-year prison term. A campaign for clemency began immediately, and thousands of Americans and Europeans wrote letters, signed petitions, held protest meetings, and pleaded with Illinois governor Richard Ogelsby to pardon the men. The governor did commute the sentences of two of the men, but the other five were condemned to die. One "outwitted the gallows by biting a percussion cap and blowing off his head," but the other four were hanged in 1887. When funerals were held after the executions, "Thousands of workers marched behind the black hearses, not because they were anarchists but they felt that these men, whatever their theories, were martyrs to the workers' struggle," Jones declared.

The four men were buried in Waldheim Cemetery in Chicago, where a memorial was placed in their honor in 1893. That year the Illinois governor was John Peter Altgeld, who pardoned the three survivors, saying the state never learned who threw the bomb that killed the police. In his statement, he noted that evidence showed the "police not only took sides against the men, but without any authority of law invaded and broke up peaceable meetings, and in scores of cases brutally clubbed people who were guilty of no offense whatsoever."

Enemies of labor seized on the violence at Haymarket to undermine the union movement. Companies labeled unions violent organizations and locked out employees who attempted to organize. Newspaper editorials lambasted unions and claimed that organizers were part of a conspiracy to overthrow the U.S. government. The public began to associate unionism with anarchism. This reaction against unions hurt the Knights of Labor. They suffered a steep drop in membership, from more than 700,000 in 1886 to less than 100,000 four years later.

Other problems affected the Knights. There were divisions within the organization, particularly over the goal of organizing all types of workers into one big union. Some members believed this was an unrealistic goal and broke away to become part of the newly formed American Federation of Labor (AFL), an association of twenty-five trade unions, with each union made up of skilled workers in a specific trade. The AFL followed its leader Samuel Gompers' philosophy of straightforward unionism. The AFL focused on getting its members the best treatment possible from industrialists. Gompers, who served as AFL president almost continuously until 1924, stressed working within the system, using negotiations, boycotts, and strikes to gain a larger share of company profits for workers. Shorter work days and safer working conditions also were part of the AFL agenda.

Although the AFL grew from an initial membership of 140,000 to more than a million after the turn of the century, most U.S. workers, especially the unskilled, did not belong to unions in the late 1800s. Efforts to organize them continued, and Jones was among the organizers. But she stayed in the background, for the most part, until the United Mine Workers of America (UMW) was founded in 1890. Led by John Mitchell, the new union became an affiliate of the AFL.

After the UMW formed, Mitchell offered Jones a paid position—five hundred dollars per year—as an organizer. She accepted, and Mitchell soon sent her to unionize miners in the coalfields of Virginia, West Virginia, Pennsylvania, and Tennessee.

4.

Organizing Workers

Mary Jones was in Tennessee in 1891 when the Tennessee Coal Mine Company tried to pressure miners to sign a contract promising not to strike. Further, the contract said, they would be paid in scrip—certificates the company provided in lieu of cash that could only be used in company stores. Miners were also told they would no longer be able to check the weight of the coal they mined. Since miners were paid a flat fee per ton of coal mined, many were reluctant to allow company officials to determine the weight of the coal. Not surprisingly, the miners refused to sign such a contract, and the company leased convicts to work the mine instead.

In the South after the Civil War, the convict-labor system was a brutal form of punishment, a source of revenue for states, and a way to control newly freed slaves. Southern states leased convicts, most of them African Americans, to plantation owners and industries. These forced laborers lived in inhumane conditions and for the least infraction received beatings with leather whips, some of them studded with pegs. In Tennessee, convict laborers in the mines died at a high rate, but there were always more convicts to replace the dead.

Miners hated the convict-labor system, and when prisoners were brought in during a strike, bedlam usually ensued. At the Tennessee coal mine, miners armed themselves, took over the mine, and freed the convicts. The company eventually agreed not to use convict labor again. In fact, after years of strikes in Tennessee mines and other industries that used convict labor, the state was forced to abolish the lease system.

Tennessee was just one of the many places Jones traveled to as a union organizer. At each stop, she lodged with workers and their families, eating with them and often sleeping on the floor with only her purse as a pillow. Jones was on the move so often and so engrossed in her work that she had little time to socialize, although she counted among her friends many union members and sympathizers across the country. Though she never remarried, some historians have speculated that she and Terence Powderly, who headed the Knights of Labor, might have had an intimate relationship, but it is impossible to determine. Powderly and his wife, Emma, often helped Jones when she needed funds or a place to stay.

Terence Powderly, leader of the Knights of Labor during the union's 1886 peak and longtime friend of Mother Jones. (Department of Labor)

While mining families usually were eager to accept help from Jones, some were afraid to offer her food and lodging because they feared retribution from company owners and management. Jones was fearless and confronted armed company guards with wisecracks and defiant remarks. She expressed contempt for bosses, managers, and owners, calling them slave masters, feudal lords, despots, robbers, and murderers. Jones relished deriding the pluck-me store or the pluck-me pay—grocery stores or utilities and other services were plucked (deducted) from miners' wages before they ever saw a penny of the money they had earned.

Mary Harris Jones, photographed here around the time she began to be known as Mother Jones. (Library of Congress)

It was during this period that people began to refer to Mary Jones as Mother Jones. She began to use the moniker for herself during speeches and when signing letters. She also constantly referred to miners as her "boys." She exaggerated her age by appearing on platforms and dressing in a matronly black dress and hat at strikes—a successful attempt to gain sympathy and respect. She also knew how to put her audiences in good humor with jokes and music, sometimes scheduling a brass band to play before she delivered a speech. Always a storyteller, she liked to use dialogue in her speeches and tales about her labor activities, giving listeners the impression that she was at the center of whatever scene she played out for her audience. By focusing on herself, Jones made audiences realize that if an elderly woman could take action, so could they. Her understanding of theatrics contributed to her success as a labor organizer.

Jones not only organized for unions, but she also assisted with raising funds for the unemployed. During the spring of 1894, she collected money and food for a group the press referred to as Coxey's Army. Jacob Coxey, a religious businessman and reformer from Ohio, organized a march of unemployed workers to be held in Washington, DC, to demand help from Congress. Coxey called those who joined his march the Army of the Commonweal of Christ, and he believed that his army would convince Congress to fund a public-works program, creating jobs to improve highways across the United States.

Coxey's Army of unemployed workers makes its way from Massillon, Ohio, to Washington, DC, in April of 1894. Among the marchers was American writer Jack London. (Courtesy of the Granger Collection.)

Mother Jones, as a champion of unemployed workers, joined a group of marchers traveling through Missouri. She gave speeches and raised money. During an overnight stop in Kansas City, the leader of her group ran off with the money that had been collected. Still, the men continued the march, although no one knows how far they got. Only a few hundred of Coxey's Army actually reached the nation's capitol, where Coxey attempted to make an emotional speech. But police did not allow him to deliver a word of his prepared remarks. He was arrested for trespassing on the Capitol lawn and sentenced to a short jail term for violating a local ordinance. Although Coxey was seen by some as a lunatic or fanatic, his march did bring national attention to the dire needs of the unemployed.

About the same time that Coxey's Army was marching to Washington, another labor disturbance was taking place near Chicago at the Pullman Palace Car Company, which manufactured railroad sleeping and parlor cars. As the economic depression had taken hold, company owner George Pullman had laid off more than half of his workers and cut wages for those remaining by 25 to 40 percent. But Pullman did not reduce the rents and other charges for workers who lived in Pullman, Illinois, a company town in which Pullman owned the homes, churches, schools, and stores where workers had to buy their food and other necessities.

Even though Pullman employees worked in manufacturing, they belonged to the American Railway Union (ARU), which had a national membership of 150,000, making it the nation's largest union. The ARU was founded in 1893 by Eugene V. Debs, who began work on the railroads when he was a young teenager. In his early adult years, he became the national secretary of the Brotherhood of Locomotive Firemen and was known as a spokesman for labor issues. He also became involved in politics and, eventually, after studying Socialist philosophy in prison, became a cofounder of the Socialist Party of America. He was the party's presidential candidate five times.

With the ARU's backing, Pullman workers formed a forty-six-member committee and petitioned George

Pullman to restore workers' wages. Pullman agreed to listen to the committee, but after the men presented their case, Pullman fired three of them. Workers interpreted this as retaliation, and in the summer of 1894, Pullman workers struck. They sought support at a convention of the ARU, asking its members to quit handling Pullman cars. Most passenger trains had Pullman sleepers, so traffic stopped on rail lines across the country, and workers barricaded tracks and derailed some trains. Because mail was transported on trains, the U.S. attorney general declared the strikers were interfering with mail delivery and violating the Interstate Commerce Act

Chicago police attempt to quell a mob of rioters in order to allow a train to pass during the Pullman Strike of 1894. (Courtesy of the Granger Collection.)

American labor leader Eugene Debs. (Courtesy of the Granger Collection.)

(both federal crimes). He issued a court injunction against them, which ordered the strikers to cease and desist. An injunction was a primary weapon the government used to break up strikes and stop union organizing.

But Pullman strikers continued their actions, burning railcars and setting off riots. Federal troops eventually broke up the strike. Officials arrested Debs and other ARU leaders for conspiracy to interfere with interstate commerce and being in contempt of court. He was convicted, but he appealed to the U.S. Supreme Court (*in re Debs* 1895), arguing that the federal government did not have the constitutional authority to prevent strikes by railroad workers. In a unanimous decision, however, the Supreme Court upheld Debs' conviction, and Debs served six months in jail.

While the rail strike was under way, Mother Jones was

in Birmingham, Alabama, encouraging 8,000 United Mine Workers who had walked off the job because of wage cuts. The UMW strike began to fizzle when scabs took over the mining jobs, but the striking miners joined forces with the ARU strikers, stopping trains that carried coal to markets. Jones worked with both UMW and ARU leaders to keep the strike going. But, as in Pullman, the militia broke up the strike in Birmingham.

After Debs was released from prison, Mother Jones organized workers to greet him in Birmingham on a Sunday afternoon in 1896. She described the scene in her autobiography:

> When we got down to the station there were several thousand miners there. . . . The train pulled in and Debs got off. Those miners did not wait for the gates to open but jumped over the railing. They put him on their shoulders and marched out of the station with the crowd in line. They marched through the streets, past the railway offices, the mayor's office, the office of the chief of police. "Debs is here! Debs is here!" they shouted.

Mother Jones had arranged to hold a meeting in an opera house, but authorities now refused to let her use the building. In response, Jones sent word that the meeting would be held regardless of the consequences, and the authorities decided not to interfere. People jammed the opera house: "the aisles, the window sills, every nook and corner" were filled, "and that night the crowd heard a real sermon by a preacher [Debs] whose message was one of human brotherhood," Jones wrote.

Debs devoted the rest of his life to working people and Socialist causes. On several occasions, Mother Jones joined him on platforms to espouse Socialist views. In 1896, she also helped launch the *Appeal to Reason*, a Socialist weekly, which focused on workers' interests. The newspaper often carried stories about Mother Jones's work in the coalfields in Pennsylvania, West Virginia, Colorado, and other places. Organizing miners was the major focus of her life, and for thirty years she spent more time with them than any other laboring group.

One of Jones's greatest strengths was her ability to give striking workers courage. Strikes were hard on miners and their families; the men would get discouraged and be ready to go back to work. But Jones would hold meetings, urging miners to pledge that they would strike until they had won their demands. John Brophy, a teenage miner who later became a union leader, recalled that Jones took "a drink with the boys and spoke their idiom, including some pretty rough language when talking about the bosses. . . . She had a lively sense of humor—she could tell wonderful stories, usually at the expense of some boss, for she couldn't resist the temptation to agitate, even in a joke."

Jones also organized miners' wives. Once, in Arnot, Pennsylvania, she told a group of women to arm themselves with mops, brooms, hammers, and pails—

anything they could find. Scabs were being brought in on mule-driven wagons and Jones was determined to turn them back. The women beat on their dishpans and howled, scaring the mules. The animals "bucked and kicked the scab drivers and started off for the barn. The scabs started running down hill, followed by the army of women with their mops and pails and brooms," according to Jones. "From that day on the women kept continual watch of the mines to see that the company did not bring in scabs."

Strikebreakers, or scabs, were common during the late 1800s. There were always plenty of unemployed people ready to take any jobs they could get. If mine operators could bring in strikebreakers, companies could keep selling coal and earning profits, which gave them less incentive to negotiate with striking workers. The appearance of scabs was nearly always a recipe for violence and bloodshed.

Because there were still many nonunion miners across the United States, John Mitchell, president of the UMW, appointed Jones international organizer. Whether her new job included a pay raise is unclear, but Mitchell hoped that with Jones's help the union could bring benefits to anthracite coal miners in eastern Pennsylvania, similar to those that the miners in the western part of the state had received. Anthracite coal, which is a hard coal that burns with a clean flame, was increasingly in demand for businesses and homes. Anthracite miners believed they deserved a pay raise and sought to have

Miners in Pennsylvania perform the exhausting work of breaking up lumps of anthracite coal with hammers. In order for anthracite to burn most efficiently, it must be broken into small, nearly uniform, chunks. (Courtesy of the Granger Collection.)

the UMW represent them. But mine owners refused to negotiate with UMW leader Mitchell.

In the middle of 1902, the anthracite miners asked Mitchell to call a special convention of the union. The miners wanted the UMW to consider a strike of all coal miners to support the anthracite miners. Jones was invited to address the convention, held in Indianapolis, Indiana. Even though she knew that Mitchell preferred negotiations rather than strikes to achieve the union's goals, Mother Jones urged action and unity. In her words, "it is solidarity of labor we want. We do not want to find fault with each other, but to solidify our forces and say to each other: 'we must be together; our masters are joined together and we must do the same thing.'"

In the end, Mitchell refused to call a general strike, but the anthracite miners decided to act on their own: they walked out en masse. In the Great Anthracite Strike of 1902, more than 150,000 miners refused to work. The strike began in May and went on into October; many Americans worried about a coal shortage in the winter. There was hope that President Theodore Roosevelt would intervene.

Roosevelt had been vice president and became president in 1901 after an assassin shot President William McKinley. Even before Roosevelt took office, the nation was experiencing the early years of what became known as the Progressive Era. Progressives called for social and economic reforms. They were helped by

President Theodore Roosevelt (left) and UMW leader John Mitchell (right) pose with a reverend not long after the anthracite strike. (Library of Congress)

"muckrakers"—reporters and others who raked up "dirt" on business corruption—who shed light on the dark side of capitalism. Ida Tarbell, for example, exposed the deliberate way the Standard Oil monopoly destroyed competition, and Jacob Riis described the pitiful life of children in New York City slums. Well-known literary figures of the day also were highly critical of capitalism and wrote about Socialists' idealized life of cooperatively owned and shared resources. One of the most famous of these writers was Upton Sinclair, whose book *The Jungle* describes the unsanitary conditions in the meat-packing industry and the inhumane treatment of working people. Another was Jack London, a young Socialist who wrote numerous adventure novels and had joined Coxey's Army in its march on Washington, DC.

Roosevelt believed that a president should be a leader in reform efforts. He worked for legislation that ended a common railroad company practice of allowing major oil and livestock companies to pay freight rates lower than the rates farmers and small businesses paid. Roosevelt also ordered his attorney general to file lawsuits against the giant trusts, or monopolies, which violated recently passed antitrust laws. Other reforms during his administration included a federal law requiring the inspection of meat-packing industries, motivated in part by Upton Sinclair's book.

Roosevelt did not favor unions—he disliked them—but he wanted the anthracite strike settled. He named a commission to take testimony from miners and their families and from the mine operators. The commission heard about the miners' unhealthy living conditions, their dangerous working conditions, and abuse by company guards. Mine operators countered by saying they had to be competitive and profitable, so it was necessary for them to control the workplace.

After hearing testimony that eventually filled fifty-six volumes, the commission ruled that the miners should receive a 10 percent pay increase, work only a nine-hour day, and be able to weigh the coal they mined in a fair manner. While Mitchell and the UMW agreed with the commission's verdict, more radical union members, including Mother Jones, were incensed because the union was not recognized as the miners' bargaining agent.

Jones believed that Mitchell should have continued the strike in order to achieve all the union's demands. This was the beginning of what would become a long-running dispute. At times the two saw eye to eye, but when Jones disagreed with him, she was quick to voice her criticism.

Over the years, Jones never hesitated to express her growing disgust for labor leaders in general. In her view, the heads of unions were more interested in compromise and earning praise from the public than in the struggle of the working class. She also detested their affluent lifestyles: many took expensive trips and vacations and attended social events hosted by the wealthy. In spite of her complaints about union leadership, however, she continued the struggle to organize workers and to demand that labor get its fair share.

5.

Theatrics and Politics

The Progressive Movement helped usher in many social reforms in the early twentieth century, but Mother Jones preferred to concentrate on organizing workers alone rather than working with or even acknowledging other activists of the time. Her writings and speeches included no words for Lucy Parsons, wife of one of the Haymarket Eight who, like Jones, was a tireless speaker and activist for the labor movement. She never mentioned Kate Richards O'Hare, a widely known and effective Socialist organizer, although she worked with her in the coalfields and the two apparently became friends. She never acknowledged the work of such reformers as Jane Addams and her Hull House settlement for poor immigrants living in slums, or the men and women who documented in photographs and stories the distressing ways that industrialization affected urban families, particularly children. And she gave only passing notice to the suffragists working for women's right to vote.

One of the reasons Mother Jones did not tout such prominent individuals was her bias against middle-class and wealthy people who supported reforms; she believed they had little understanding of what it meant to be part of the working class. She often said she was a working man's daughter and had experienced firsthand the struggle to survive. Because she was contemptuous of those who accumulated material things, she lived simply. She had little money, no home of her own, and traveled by rail, sometimes with the help of sympathetic trainmen who let her on board free of charge. In short, Jones set her sights on a specific goal: organizing workers so they could improve their lives.

It was a grueling task. Wherever Jones and her organizers went, they met vicious resistance from company officials, their guards, and lawmen. Repeatedly, she and the miners had to deal with coal company thugs such as those at the Fairmont Coal Company in West Virginia.

During the Fairmont strike there were many attacks on striking workers. Some were shot dead in their beds. But the brutality did not damage organizational efforts as much as the injunctions issued by Judge John Jackson. He forbid organizers to meet in schools, churches, or other public buildings. When Jones and her coworkers defied his orders, police arrested them.

In court, the prosecuting attorney, who questioned Jones for hours, called her the "most dangerous woman in America," because she was able to convince miners to stop working. But the attorney did not intimidate Jones, and she frequently conversed with the judge as if she had known him all her life, sometimes even joking with him. When someone in the court admonished her to address the judge as "your honor," she retorted, "Well, I can't call him 'your honor' until I know how honorable he is. You know I took an oath to tell the truth when I took the witness stand."

The judge told Jones that if she left the state and would "be a good girl generally," he would not bother her anymore. But true to form, Jones said "I asked my lawyer to tell him . . . all the devils in hell would not get me out of West Virginia. . . . I was there to stay, and if I died in West Virginia in jail it made no difference with my decision."

Judge Jackson sentenced six of Jones's coworkers to sixty days and one to ninety days in jail, but he suspended Jones's sentence, saying he did not want to make a martyr of her. The judge scolded Jones for being used by "reckless agitators" and said, "It would have been far better for her to follow the lines and paths which the Allwise Being intended her sex to pursue." He declared that she should contribute to charities "as well as avocations and pursuits . . . that would be more in keeping with what . . . experience has shown to be the true sphere of womanhood."

Jones was not about to be chastised without having her say. In her melodramatic and humorous way, she informed the judge that they were both getting very old (by her account she was in her seventies) and she hoped some day they would meet again in heaven. Before then, she expected to be arrested once more—or several times, if that was what was in store for her—as she continued the fight for workers.

One group of workers Jones felt particularly responsible for was children. Other Progressives also championed the cause of ending child labor. Laboring at a young age ruined the health and lives of countless children, but many poor families relied on the small sums their children earned. The few pennies they brought home could provide a meal. The argument that they were actually helping poor families by hiring their children was sometimes used by the owners, but it was dismissed by Jones and other reformers. They were adamant in their view that it was a moral duty to protect young children and to educate them.

Jones had seen youngsters who worked in the mines whose lungs were ruined by coal dust that caused chronic respiratory problems. Many became stooped and malformed because of twelve-hour shifts hauling huge baskets or carts of coal. Boys as young as six or seven worked illegally as coal breakers. They sat by coal chutes, and when coal poured through, they picked out rocks and slate that would not burn. A breaker boss kept watch, hitting the boys on the knuckles if they did not

Breaker boys, as they were known, toil next to the coal chutes. The young boys labored in near darkness, the coal dust so dense at times that it would obscure their work. (Library of Congress)

keep pace. The boss cared little if boys lost their balance and fell into the chute, where they could be severely injured or killed.

Industrialists in the South and North hired children to work in mines and also in steel and textile mills and factories. The young workers were fast, agile, and easier to control than adults. Many children started work anywhere from age eight to twelve. John L. Davis, who went on to become U.S. secretary of labor, was one of those child laborers, starting in an iron and steel mill when he was twelve years old. In his later years he described how he melted pig iron in intense heat:

Vigorously I stoked that fire for thirty minutes with dampers open and the draft roaring while that pig-iron melted down like ice cream under an electric fan. . . . There were five bakings every day and this meant the shoveling in of nearly two tons of coal. In summer I was stripped to the waist and panting while the sweat poured down. . . . My palms and fingers, scorched by the heat, became hardened like goat hoofs, while my skin took on a coat of tan that it will wear forever.

While organizing miners, Mother Jones heard stories about the dreadful working conditions for children in cotton mills in the South. At first, she thought the tales were exaggerations, so she decided to investigate, getting a job at a Cottondale, Alabama mill and staying with workers in their homes. In an article for the *International Socialist Review,* she reported six- and seven-year-old children were being "dragged out of bed at half-past 4 in the morning when the task-master's whistle blew." After a "scanty meal of black coffee and corn bread," an "army of serfs, big and little" trotted off.

By 5:30, they are all behind the factory walls, where amid the whir of machinery they grind their young lives out for fourteen long hours each day. . . . I have seen mothers take their babes and slap cold water in their face to wake the poor little things. I have watched them all day long tending the dangerous machinery. I have seen their helpless limbs torn off, and then when they were disabled and of no more use to their master, thrown out to die.

Jones also went to a rope factory in Tuscaloosa, Alabama, where children worked in lint and dust. Many suffered from bronchitis or other lung ailments and some died of pneumonia. Some were killed working around the spindles, including a young girl whose hair was caught in a whirring machine, scalping her. She was dead at eleven years old.

In her article, Jones condemned a capitalist system

Young girls, one a "raveler" and the other a "looper," at work during their shift at the Loudon Hosiery Mill in Tennessee, 1910. (Library of Congress)

that allowed child labor. She saw the industrial system as one of "torture and murder," writing, "I shudder for the future of the nation that is building up a moneyed aristocracy out of the life-blood of the children of the proletariat [working class]. . . . The whole picture is one of the most horrible avarice, selfishness and cruelty."

After her experience in the mills, Jones wrote that she "was burdened with the terrible things I had seen. . . . I could scarcely eat." In her view, her clothes as well as her food "at times seemed bought with the price of the toil of children." She tried to get public and political attention to focus on the problem of child labor.

In 1903, she thought she would have an opportunity when about 75,000 textile workers, more than 10,000 of them children under the age of sixteen, went out on strike in the Kensington district of Philadelphia, Pennsylvania. Jones came up with a plan to create publicity. She arranged a parade to a public square opposite city hall. There, on a platform, she put youngsters who had been injured. Holding up the children's maimed arms or lifting them high so all could see their scrawny frames, Jones excoriated the crowd that had gathered. "Philadelphia's mansions were built on [the] broken bones, the quivering hearts and drooping heads of these children," she scolded.

Jones's street theater brought some public attention to the plight of child workers. But the focus soon wavered, and Jones decided on another course of action. Similar to the protest made by Coxey's Army, she planned to organize child workers and adult helpers to march from Philadelphia to President Roosevelt's vacation home at Oyster Bay on Long Island, New York. Jones wanted the president to urge Congress to pass legislation banning child labor.

At first, the public and some striking textile workers derided the march. But as the group of several hundred moved along its dusty route in the hot summer, reporters covered their progress and the speeches Jones made at meeting places and rest stops. Some of the children had to drop out because of the heat and their poor health. But even though their numbers dwindled, the marchers continued to gain attention.

As the strikers pushed on, they were supported by Socialist groups, such as the Socialist Party of Elizabeth, New Jersey, and the Social Democratic Party in New York City. The marchers stayed for two days at the Socialist headquarters in New York. They spent another two relaxing days at Coney Island at the invitation of an animal trainer. While at the amusement park, Jones— ever mindful of theatrics—put some children in empty animal cages and told a crowd that the young workers represented the way mine and mill owners treated their most vulnerable employees.

Three weeks after the march began, the Children's Crusade, as it was called, only numbered a few dozen, but it had reached Oyster Bay. President Roosevelt refused to meet with Mother Jones or to see the children. Obviously that was a disappointment, but even more disheartening was the fact that in order to survive, the textile workers were forced to go back to work, ending the strike without gaining benefits.

Nevertheless, the march was an important first step toward reforms. A year later, the National Child Labor Committee (NCLC) formed, and a few years later, Congress authorized the committee to investigate all types of child labor. The NCLC issued a report that described numerous examples of the way children were employed. In addition, the committee hired photographer Lewis Hines to document the plight of children at work. His haunting pictures dramatically revealed the wretchedness of children working in mills, mines, canneries, and other industries. This publicity convinced some state legislatures to pass laws to protect children. But most states had only a few inspectors, and even when companies were cited for labor-law violations, state courts often dismissed cases or levied only minor fines. At the federal level, no significant laws banning child labor were passed until years after Mother Jones died.

While Jones kept up her campaign to ban child labor, unionism in general was growing and strikes were planned or under way in other industries besides mining, from breweries to garment manufacturing to transportation. Jones toiled at a feverish pace, organizing workers, speaking out against capitalism, and promoting socialism. The Socialist Party tried to convince Jones that she should work full time for them, but in the fall of 1903, she was still with the United Mine Workers. Union leaders meeting in Indianapolis, Indiana, asked Jones to go to Colorado and investigate conditions at the south-central coalfields of the Colorado Fuel and Iron Company.

Miners in the south-central coalfields of Colorado were organized by the militant Western Federation of Miners (WFM), who endorsed socialism and represented gold, silver, and lead miners and smelters, and some coal miners in the northern area. The WFM had already won an eight-hour work day for its miners, but in early 1901, the manager of a coal mine in the Telluride district of southwestern Colorado set up a system whereby workers were paid by the amount of coal they mined rather than by the hours they worked each day. To the miners, this was an attempt to destroy the eight-hour day, and the union went on strike. It was the beginning of a long conflict, pitting the WFM against the mining and rail monopolies, the state government, and the militia, all of whom attempted to destroy unionism. Both sides armed for a fight.

When Mother Jones went to Colorado in the fall of 1903, the WMF metal miners and smelters were striking in the northern area and wanted coal miners to join them. But coal miners in Colorado's southern fields seemed powerless. The company owned everything—the land, roads, houses, stores, schools, and even the churches. Jones advised the UMW officials to call a strike of Colorado coal miners, and the strike began in early November 1903. But a few weeks later, Jones learned that miners in the northern coalfields were planning to

Mother Jones marches the streets of Trinidad, Colorado, during her 1903 visit to support the Western Federation of Miners. (Newberry Library, Chicago)

call off their strike because the mine owners had met their demands. John Mitchell, president of the UMW, supported the settlement and ordered Jones not to interfere. But she rushed to the scene and, in a powerful address at a mass meeting, urged the miners to stand firm and not to compromise with mine operators. She believed all miners should be united in the strike, and miners in the north should support those in the south. In her view, solidarity was the only way that all miners could win.

According to a report in the *Denver Post,* Jones

> began her speech in a low conversational tone. . . . She was quiet and calm at first and smiled now and then, and as she made a humorous reference to the

situation or scored a hit on the operators....She did not waste much time with quiet speech. She soon raised her voice to a pitch of fervid eloquence. . . .The men responded to every appeal with enthusiasm.

Jones won the men over to her cause, and they voted to refuse to go back to work. This was the first major defeat for John Mitchell. Mitchell sent UMW officials to convince the miners who wanted to end the strike to go along with their national leaders. The miners held another vote to reconsider, and this time the majority voted to go back to work.

Jones was livid. According to her, the northern miners had "created practical peonage in the south." Although the strike went on for another year, the southern Colorado miners lost. Jones decried the fact that they had suffered for nothing, living in tents "with eighteen inches of snow on the ground. They tied their feet in gunny sacks and lived lean and lank and hungry as timber wolves . . . while John Mitchell went traveling through Europe, staying at fashionable hotels, studying the labor movement." After the strike was over, Mitchell and other UMW leaders did go to an international meeting of miners in Paris, France, and looked at mining operations in several European countries.

Jones claimed that because of her criticism of Mitchell, "the guns were turned on me. Slander and persecution followed me like black shadows." Indeed rumors circulated that because of her rough talk and close association with beer-drinking miners, she must be a wicked woman. Some people alleged that she had once operated a house of prostitution, but no evidence was presented.

The Colorado governor tried to run Jones out of the state. But she stayed, and traveled to the southern mining area where there was continued unrest and violence. Traveling and campaigning began to take a toll on her health. She became ill with pneumonia and was hospitalized in Trinidad, Colorado, early in 1904. When she was able to leave the hospital, Socialist and union friends took her into their homes and helped her regain her health. While recuperating she began to consider the job offer made earlier by the Socialist Party.

Mother Jones had become increasingly frustrated with John Mitchell and his tactics. She decided to resign her position as international organizer at the UMW and become a Socialist lecturer. She was paid three dollars a day. Local Socialist groups covered her expenses as she traveled from city to city to give speeches.

In 1905, she and other Socialists and radicals took part in the formation of the Industrial Workers of the World (IWW), a union commonly known as the Wobblies. The IWW was not an industry-specific union of skilled laborers. Its goal was to represent the working class around the world and to organize unskilled and skilled workers to launch a worldwide general strike that would destroy the power of factory owners and put workers in control of their own destinies.

What was called a secret Continental Congress of the

Working Class convened in Chicago in January to discuss ways to organize the working class. IWW organizers hoped to unite working women as well as men, and workers from all racial backgrounds. Most unions of the day, such as those affiliated with the AFL, barred blacks and other people of color from membership. IWW also advocated direct action—that is, workers themselves, not union leaders, initiating, controlling, and settling a strike.

Jones was the only woman among the three dozen radicals that attended the initial meeting. Six months later, a founding convention was held, and twelve women were among the delegates, including Mother Jones. Chair of the convention was William "Big Bill" Haywood, a Western Federation of Miners official and member of the Socialist Party, who declared that the IWW would "confederate the workers of this country into a working class movement that shall have for its purpose the emancipation of the working class from the slave bondage of capitalism."

In a preamble to its constitution, the IWW stated:

> The working class and the employing class have nothing in common. There can be no peace so long as hunger and want are found among millions of working people and the few, who make up the employing class, have all the good things of life. Between these two classes a struggle must go on until workers of the world organize as a class, take possession of the means of production, abolish the wage system, and live in harmony with the Earth.

William Dudley "Big Bill" Haywood, former miner, union leader, and eventual founding member of the International Workers of the World. (Library of Congress)

For about six years, from 1905 to 1911, Jones spread the Socialist message. She also wrote for Socialist publications and distributed Socialist pamphlets. Yet she was not a formal member of the Socialist Party, even though years earlier she had helped organize the Social Democratic Party, which later became the Socialist Party of America. In fact, at times she would criticize members of the Socialist Party just as she found fault with the Western Federation of Miners and the United Mine Workers of America. Other times, she supported their causes. In other words, she had independent views, and consistently expressed her opinion in colorful, melo-dramatic language.

Some of Jones's most stinging barbs were aimed at the clergy and churches. Although she proclaimed Christian beliefs and used biblical references in her speeches to workers, she criticized churches for taking up collections for people in other lands but ignoring the poor in their own congregations. She once wrote to fellow Socialist Jack London, whom she addressed as "Comrade," complaining that the "church bell tolls each Easter morning and announces the resurrection of the Christ. . . . [but] it has never tolled for the resurrection of Christ's children from their long dark tomb of slavery." In Jones's view, the union, not the clergy, was doing God's work and was on a moral mission to improve the lives of laborers.

6.

Imprisoned

In spite of her exhausting travel and her differences with John Mitchell, Mother Jones took time out to attend UMW conventions and speak to delegates. But she did not always lecture about the mining industry. One of her concerns focused on raising funds for Mexican rebels who had fled to the United States to escape the brutal dictatorship of Mexican president Porfirio Díaz; the revolutionaries were intent on bringing about land and social reforms in Mexico.

In 1909, Jones went before the UMW convention to ask for money on the rebels' behalf. She told the delegates about U.S. authorities kidnapping Mexican rebel Manuel Sarabia and turning him over to Mexican police, who imprisoned him. There was little doubt that he would be killed. Other revolutionaries were also jailed

Armed Mexican insurgents stand guard at their outpost during the 1910 revolution that ousted Porfirio Díaz from power. (Library of Congress)

in the United States, awaiting deportation. Jones argued that they should be protected just as people from countries such as Ireland and Russia had found refuge in the United States from tyrannical governments.

"We have got to get those boys out of jail," Jones told the delegates. "We have got to let them live in this land; we have got to let them fight Mexico from here." She blamed U.S. corporations and a "Canadian and British syndicate" that owned "railroads and street cars and the land" given to them for their part in exploiting Mexican workers. Jones showed pictures of Mexican miners who had attempted to strike and were found hanged "with their flesh eaten off their bodies."

Not only did Mother Jones succeed in convincing the UMW to donate money for the defense of the jailed refugees, she also raised funds from other groups and continued her publicity efforts and appeals to U.S. government authorities to help free Sarabia. The protests played an important role in liberating Sarabia and getting him back to the United States.

The "Mexican question," as Jones called it, prompted a Congressional hearing in 1910, and Jones was summoned to appear. When a Congressman asked her to tell the panel where she lived, she replied with a now-famous remark: "My address is like my shoes, it travels with me." She explained further, "My address is wherever there is a fight against oppression." Jones proceeded to describe her efforts for the Mexican revolutionaries in her compelling style:

> Gentlemen, in the name of our own Revolutionary heroes, in the name of the heroes unborn, in the name of those whose statues stand silently in Statuary Hall, I beg that this body of representatives will protect these Mexican men from the tyranny of this bloody tyrant, Díaz.

In an article for *Appeal to Reason,* Jones called on "Brothers and Comrades" to "stand for freedom, right and justice" in the case of the Mexican revolutionaries. She declared that Díaz had "given American capitalists concessions that are worth millions of dollars, and guarantees them peon labor that dare not ask higher wages under penalty of being shot for violating the law; and in return he asks that if political refugees escape to

America, or if a Mexican dare to come to America and criticize him, they must be returned to him, that they may be shot."

By the middle of 1911, a revolution had succeeded in overthrowing Díaz, who escaped to Europe. The new president granted workers the right to organize, and Jones earned praise and gratitude for her efforts to prevent U.S. imprisonment of Mexican rebels.

While agitating to resolve the "Mexican question," Mother Jones also took action to help working women. Between 1909 and 1910, the nation's first significant strike of working women took place in New York City.

Mexican dictator Porfirio Díaz, who eventually died in exile in Paris in 1915. (Library of Congress)

The strike began in two large shirtwaist shops—Leiserson & Company and the Triangle Waist Company—where workers made a popular high-necked blouse for women. Conditions in these and other such shops were miserable. The buildings were grimy and without ventilation—windows were locked shut. Most of the workers were immigrant Jewish and Italian women, fifteen to twenty-five years old with limited English skills. They needed the work to survive, but their wages, about six dollars per week, barely provided necessities. The young women worked twelve hours a day, seven days each week. In some shops, the women had to use their own needles and thread, and, on occasion, their own sewing machines. Bosses fined workers if they talked or laughed or if they damaged fabrics.

The International Ladies Garment Workers' Union (ILGWU) and the Women's Trade Union League (WTUL) had slowly organized some of the women, and they went out on strike in September 1909. In November, workers held a mass meeting to determine whether to call a general strike against shirtwaist manufacturers. A general strike would involve most waistmakers in the city. The discussion went on for hours, until Clara Lemlich, a young woman who had been in earlier strikes, stood up and declared:

> I am a working girl, and one of those who are on strike against intolerable conditions. I am tired of listening to speakers who talk in general terms. What we are here for is to decide whether or not we

Strikers during the garment workers strike in New York City in February 1910.
(Library of Congress)

will strike. I offer a resolution that a general strike
be declared—now!

The crowd responded enthusiastically, which led to
the walkout of an estimated 20,000 to 30,000 shirtwaist
workers in nearly five hundred shops in New York City.

In December, Mother Jones spoke to the strikers in
New York. Sponsored by the local Socialist Party, the
meeting was held in a theater, and Jones began her
address with "This is not a play, this is a fight!" She went
on to tell her audience:

> You make all the fine waists, but you do not wear
> them. . . . You ought to parade past the shops where
> you work and up the avenue where the swells who
> wear the waists you made live. They won't like to
> see you, they will be afraid of you!

Mother Jones urged the strikers to stick together and to fight "for the time when there will be no master and no slave." The strike went on for thirteen weeks, under terrible conditions. Police constantly attacked picketers with clubs, arrested them, and jailed them in filthy cells. Strikers, however, gained support from the public and financial help from wealthy patrons and were able to hold out. By February, many factory owners had agreed to higher wages, shorter work hours, and recognition of the union. Nevertheless, it was only a partial victory. Strikers wanted a closed shop, which would mean hiring only union members, and most shop owners refused to even discuss such a thing.

Although Jones rallied workers with her powerful speehes, her true passion was to organize, an action the Socialist Party did not openly support. As this became more clear, Jones began to clash with the Socialists. One member accused her of being an alcoholic, and another revived rumors that she had once run a brothel. Jones vehemently denied the accusations, and her old friend Eugene Debs staunchly defended her. But the breaking point had come, and although each side had a different version of the story— whether she was thrown out or whether she quit—Jones left the Socialist Party in 1911.

The break was bitter and came at a time when the Socialists were making significant inroads, but Jones could not remain a part of an organization she felt was too far removed from the working class and its struggle. She returned to the UMW.

The next year, Jones went to the West Virginia coalfields sandwiched between two streams—Paint and Cabin Creeks—in the Kanawha River Valley. Most of the Paint Creek miners were union members. Union leaders hoped to negotiate with owners for a small pay raise, but mine operators refused to grant the increase. When operators also refused to recognize the union as the workers' bargaining agent, miners, including nonunion workers, went out on strike. The company retaliated by forcing miners and their families out of company houses. Families had to set up tents for shelter near Cabin Creek.

The strike soon spread to the Cabin Creek mines, where there was no union representation. As Jones wrote, "The miners had been peons for years, kept in slavery by the guns of the coal company, and by the system of paying in scrip so that a miner never had any money should he wish to leave."

Jones's statement was not an exaggeration. Guards set up machine guns at various places and patrolled the company roads with rifles ready to keep organizers out of the valley. Like the miners at Paint Creek, striking Cabin Creek workers were forced to live in a tent colony. Gunmen intimidated families with beatings and killings, and many miners armed themselves to fight back.

Mother Jones helps out with the children in a West Virginia mine camp near Cabin Creek. (Newberry Library, Chicago)

Determined to encourage miners to continue their walkout, the elderly Mother Jones, now in her seventies or early eighties, went to volatile Cabin Creek. Miners asked her to speak to a group at a mountain camp and sent a mule-drawn buggy to transport her. Jones had to travel along the creek bed because, she reported, "that was the only public road and I could be arrested for trespass if I took any other." Coal companies owned all the roads in the area.

On the way, she encountered guards who stood behind machine guns, threatening to shoot her and the miners with her. She confronted one guard, placing her hand over the muzzle of his gun and said, "If you shoot one bullet out of this gun at those men, if you touch one of my white hairs, that creek will run with blood." She pointed up toward the hills and said there were hundreds of miners in the mountains "marching armed to the meeting I am going to address. If you start the shooting, they will finish the game." The miners and Mother Jones were allowed to pass by without incident. In reality, there were no armed men waiting to attack, only "a few jack rabbits, perhaps," Jones wrote. Her bluff had worked.

Jones also brought miners together outside the strike zone at public meetings in West Virginia towns, and at the capitol building and public square in Charleston. In her addresses to crowds, she often shook her raised fist and berated company owners who exploited workers and government officials who served the wealthy. She peppered her speeches with profanity and derisive terms for the exploiters: "bloodsuckers," "pirates," "murderers," "parasites," and "tyrants" were some of her favorites.

The Paint and Cabin Creek strikes went on for months and became increasingly bloody. Strikers and company guards attacked and counterattacked, until West Virginia governor William Glasscock placed the strike zone under martial law and called in the militia, which disarmed both sides.

Although calm prevailed for a short time and martial law was temporarily lifted, violence flared again as the strike went on, and once again martial law was imposed. In February 1913, this pattern was repeated for the third time, and the military arrested dozens of miners and strike sympathizers. At the time, Mother Jones was on her way by train to Charleston to see the newly elected governor and ask for help for the miners. When she got off the train, two men grabbed her, forced her into a car, and put her on a train to a military headquarters, where she was jailed. She and forty-seven others faced charges of murder and conspiracy to commit murder stemming from the Paint and Cabin Creek strike.

Because the military had taken control in the strike zone, Jones and the rest were tried before a military court. On the advice of their lawyers, most of them refused to plead guilt or innocence, instead denying the authority of the court to try them. The evidence against Jones was rather thin, consisting mainly of speeches she made exhorting strikers to protect themselves and their families (though in those same speeches she also told them to remain calm and stay within the law). The court appeared to be trying to make a point by targeting strike leaders. It is unclear whether Jones was convicted (the court's records were destroyed), but that seems likely since she remained under guard while other prisoners were released. The military held her in solitary confinement in a room of a boarding house, guarded night and day by soldiers outside her door. Typically, Jones was friendly with the soldiers, even convincing one to sneak her out so they could have drinks at a local pub.

The military kept news reports under strict control, and news of Mother Jones's imprisonment did not leak out until Fremont Older, the editor of a San Francisco newspaper, sent his wife to interview her. Cora Older wrote an article for *Collier's Magazine* and reported Jones's ordeal to U.S. Senator John Kern, who began efforts to organize a congressional inquiry. Others, including Eugene Debs, wrote articles for *Appeal to Reason* and other Socialist publications, calling for Jones's release. Even people with no ties to unions expressed indignation over the treatment of the miners and Mother Jones.

West Virginia Governor Henry D. Hatfield and the UMW worked out a strike settlement in April 1913, but Mother Jones was still confined. By May, a congressional investigation of the armed conflict in West Virginia was under way, and it generated so much publicity that Governor Hatfield was forced to free Jones and most of the other remaining prisoners.

Not long after her release, Jones traveled west to the Colorado Fuel and Iron Corporation mines owned by the Rockefeller family. John D. Rockefeller had developed an empire that included oil companies and coal mines. After he retired, his son John Jr. (often called Junior) was put in charge of about two dozen Colorado mines. As in other mines across the country, Colorado mines were dangerous places, but fatal accidents in Colorado were higher than in any other state. More than 460 miners were killed or injured statewide in 1913. Like his father, Rockefeller Jr. hated unions, and was convinced that the open shop was a sacred ideal. An open shop meant that workers did not have to join a union.

In earlier years, Jones had been to Colorado several times to organize, and had been arrested, jailed, and deported from the state. At a convention in the fall of 1913, she spoke to southern Colorado miners whose conditions were like those that led to walkouts in West Virginia. Jones urged them, "Rise up and strike! If you are too cowardly to fight for your rights, there are enough women in this country to come in and beat hell out of you. If it is slavery or strike, I say strike until the last one of you drop into your graves." The miners voted for a strike, which meant being forced out of their homes and enduring terrible hardships.

As in West Virginia, the strikers lived in tents. The largest campground was near Ludlow, Colorado, and consisted of more than one thousand people of varied nationalities—immigrants from Greece, Italy, Serbia, and more than a dozen other countries. Guards hired by mining companies regularly attacked the colonies. The strikers fought back and deaths mounted on both sides.

As the strike went on into the winter months, Mother Jones tried many ways to get help, going to Washington, DC, to talk to members of Congress, and to New York, Boston, and Seattle to raise money for the strike. While she was gone, mine owners convinced Colorado governor Elias Ammons to send in the militia and to keep Jones out of Colorado.

Mother Jones scoffed at the very idea she could not travel freely and returned to Colorado. Ammons sent state troops to arrest her. She was kept for nine weeks at a Sisters of Charity hospital, a portion of which the military turned into a prison. When Jones was finally released, Governor Ammons ordered her to stay out of the strike zone. But back she went, and again authorities arrested her.

This time she was held in a prison that had been declared unfit for humans. Her cell was in the basement of the county court house in Walsenburg, Colorado. "It was a cold, terrible place, without heat, damp and dark," Jones reported in her autobiography. "I slept in my clothes by day, and at night I fought great sewer rats with a beer bottle. For twenty-six days I was held a military prisoner in that black hole." She could not speak to anyone, read any publication, or make any contact with the outside world. Authorities never charged Jones with a crime.

A miner's wife in the Ludlow tent colony during the brutal winter of 1913. (Courtesy of the Denver Public Library.)

Colorado women march in protest of Mother Jones's imprisonment and in support of the workers at Ludlow. (Courtesy of the Denver Public Library.)

As word of Mother Jones's illegal captivity leaked out, publicity about her situation spread across the land.

Her supporters wrote to members of Congress, U.S. President Woodrow Wilson, and other government officials in the U.S. Departments of Justice and Labor. One group of Colorado women called for the impeachment of Governor Ammons and demanded freedom for Mother Jones. The women declared, "If the men of the state of Colorado are going to stand idly by and see the motherhood of this state plundered, profaned, and disinherited, then we, the women of Colorado, shall . . . take whatever actions are necessary to secure the liberation of Mother Jones, the abolition of military despotism, and the restoration of the constitution to the people of Colorado."

A UMW lawyer was able to obtain a writ of habeas corpus, which allows anyone imprisoned to have a court proceeding to determine whether her or his detention is legal. Jones would appear in the Colorado Supreme Court. Worried that the proceedings would not be favorable for them and would provide even more national publicity for Mother Jones, military authorities freed her, and she traveled to Washington, DC, to testify before a congressional hearing about the Colorado strike.

Rockefeller Jr. also testified at the hearing, claiming that the miners' working conditions were just fine. Under cross examination, however, he admitted he had not actually been to the mines in a decade. Junior had placed his faith in the mine's manager, LaMont Bowers. The events to come would make Rockefeller regret his hands-off style.

7.

More Battles

During the time Mother Jones was in Washington, DC, violent attacks between the Rockefeller company guards and strikers in Colorado continued. Guards kidnapped union organizers to intimidate them. Sometimes they would tell strikers that they would be shot and would have to dig their own graves. But just as strikers thought they were about to be killed, the guards would laugh and send them off with a beating.

Adding to the conflict, the Colorado governor called out the militia, which was supplemented by troops hired by the coal companies. The militia was sent to stations overlooking the Ludlow tent colony. In the camp, families had dug pits (like bunkers or foxholes) inside their tents and hidden there for protection when gunfire flared—which was often. Guards would harass strikers by firing at random into the tents. One young boy in a tent was shot through the head while eating a meal.

On April 20, the guards circled the campground and began firing. Strikers fired back, and a battle began that went on most of the day. When the strikers ran out of ammunition, most of them escaped with their families.

That night the guards became a mob. They went on a rampage in the camp, looting and setting fire to tents. The next morning, a worker for the telephone company found the bodies of two women and eleven children in a pit where they had tried to shield themselves from gunfire, only to be asphyxiated when the tent colony burned.

News of the Ludlow Massacre, as it became known, spread rapidly, and the UMW issued a call to arms.

The massacre at Ludlow made the June 1914 cover of the monthly publication The Masses, *a Socialist journal founded in 1911 and edited by leftist writer Max Eastman. The dramatic cover image of an armed miner holding a dead child was drawn by renowned American artist John Sloan.* (Library of Congress)

Miners all over Colorado left their jobs and armed themselves. Other workers joined them, and they blew up mines and killed guards. There were demonstrations and marches across the United States.

Mother Jones took a train from Washington to Denver, Colorado, where she addressed a mass protest. As the strike continued, creating bedlam and warfare across Colorado, President Woodrow Wilson sent federal troops to restore order. UMW leaders did not dare fight the U.S. Army because of the public backlash that would follow, but they hoped that Wilson would seek arbitration— appoint an impartial person or group to settle the differences between miners and owners. That did not happen, and the Army stayed on for months.

Jones kept up a grueling schedule, giving speeches, seeking funds for the striking miners, and denouncing the power of capitalists to suppress the working class. One of the stops on her journey was a UMW convention in Pittsburg, Kansas, where she told delegates, "No time in modern history has there been anything so horrible as this trouble in Colorado." She related what she had seen among miners in Colorado and West Virginia, blaming the horrors on the government and the mine owners, especially John D. Rockefeller and his son, John Jr. She wanted the UMW delegates to increase funds for the striking miners in Colorado and for the legal defense of imprisoned strikers. The delegates voted to provide $10,000 for the Colorado UMW.

Jones made similar fund-raising speeches in various

Mother Jones speaks passionately to a crowd in this photograph featured in the December 1915 issue of the International Socialist Review. (Newberry Library, Chicago)

cities, interrupting her efforts to take trips to Washington to lobby Congress. She argued that the federal government should take over the Colorado mines to stop the bloodshed. In September 1914, with federal troops still in Colorado, President Wilson offered a plan that would establish a commission to investigate problems at the mines but included no pay raise for miners. The plan also called for an end to strikes for three years.

Because the UMW was running out of money, its leaders wanted to accept Wilson's offer. But they left that decision to district members meeting in a special convention in Trinidad, Colorado. Jones was there to support Wilson's plan—even though she had adamantly called for the miners to strike a year before. At Trinidad she insisted that bayonets and guns would have to go and that peace was essential: "The sword will have to disappear and the pen will have to take its place."

The delegates voted in favor of Wilson's proposal, but the mine operators were against it. Operators wanted the UMW out of Colorado—period. They stalled for weeks until the president actually set up an investigative commission. The long strike ended in December 1914, and the miners went back to work. But they had gained nothing. In Mother Jones's view they lost because "the other side had bayonets. In the end, bayonets always win."

Rockefeller and the mine operators did not win everything. The adverse publicity tainted the Rockefeller family name, and the strike cost the mining companies hundreds of thousands of dollars. Showing real regret for the events at Ludlow, Rockefeller hired a public relations expert to boost the company image and established what he called an industrial democracy program, carefully designed to limit the potential influence of

John D. Rockefeller Jr., who took much of the blame for the mishandling of the Ludlow strike. (Library of Congress)

unions. The plan allowed employees to elect their own nonunion representatives to meet with company officials and mediate labor issues. Announcing such a program, he said, "Capital cannot move a wheel without labor, nor can labor advance beyond a more primitive existence without capital." Rockefeller himself launched the Colorado Industrial Plan, also known as the Rockefeller Plan, at the Colorado mines. He and his wife mixed with the miners and their families and tried to demonstrate the benefits of industrial democracy.

Unions criticized Rockefeller's plan as paternalistic, and Mother Jones called it "a sham and fraud." Nevertheless, such organizations spread to other industries with the support of the Wilson administration. But union organizing continued, strikes were still common, and Mother Jones never stopped exhorting workers and protesting unjust arrests of union organizers.

In August 1915, Jones was in Pittsburg, Kansas, and addressed a public protest over the imprisonment of two labor organizers in California who had been convicted, on flimsy evidence, of bombing the *Los Angeles Times* building. As usual Jones spoke about her varied experiences. She also had words of contempt for "Oily John," as she called Rockefeller Sr., and derided a Protestant minister who praised him as a great man for the country. Jones told her audience, "There is no doubt but what [Rockefeller Sr.] is the greatest murderer the nation had ever produced; no question about it, the greatest thief. . . . he has murdered, shot, starved, sent to an untimely grave men, women and children by the thousands . . . and if that is your modern version of Christianity may God Almighty save me from getting any of it in my system."

Interestingly, this was in contrast to statements she had made months earlier about the younger Rockefeller when she had accepted an invitation to visit him. After her visit, she said she had misjudged him and did not hold him personally responsible for the Ludlow tragedy.

While Jones at times contradicted herself or reversed her opinions in her speeches and writings, she was nonetheless consistent in her contempt for people who acted and spoke in a pious manner but had no compassion or aid for the downtrodden. Wherever she spoke, she rallied a crowd by blasting hypocrites, but she also sprinkled her speeches with humor.

At the Pittsburg meeting, she wanted to impress on her audience how easy it was to stand up and protest. She told about telephone company men who tried to install poles for telephone lines on a farmer's land. The farmer refused to let the men dig on his property. The men went away but returned with a court order to dig. So the farmer went to the barn and opened the door to let out a bull. The bull charged at the men, who quickly retreated and begged the farmer to call the animal off. As Jones told it:

> The old farmer said, "I have got nothing to do with the bull; you have got the order of the court." "Take him in, we want to work," says they. "Hell," says he, "Why don't you read the order of the court to the bull."

The audience got the point. They sent a formal protest regarding the imprisonment of California labor organizers to President Wilson.

Throughout 1915 and 1916, Mother Jones seemed to be in perpetual motion—traveling back and forth across the United States, lecturing and organizing workers and sometimes testifying before government committees. She fought for chemical workers on strike in New Jersey, iron workers striking in Michigan, striking streetcar workers in El Paso, Texas, and New York. She supported workers in the steel mills of Ohio and garment workers such as the Ladies' Waist and Dressmakers' Union in New York City and Chicago.

Industrialists and antiunion newspapers criticized Jones, accusing her of inciting violence and even taking digs at her age. Some spread rumors that she drank heavily, and one made the mistake of trying to insult her using the epithet, "the grandmother of agitators." To the last label she responded: "Thank God I have lived to be a grandmother in agitation! I hope I will live to be a great-grandmother in agitation!"

While the agitation for better industrial working conditions and pay went on, the United States was edging ever closer to entering World War I. The war to end all wars, as many believed it would be, began in Europe in 1914, with the Allies—Britain, France, Russia, Serbia and other nations—pitted against the Central Powers, which included Germany and Austria-Hungary in central Europe. Some Americans in Europe supported the Allies' effort, but most people in the United States saw no reason to be involved, and President Wilson said the United States would remain neutral.

However, in May 1915, a submarine, one of the German *Unterseeboote* (U-boats), attacked the British passenger liner *Lusitania* off the coast of Ireland. A torpedo sank the ship, and 1,195 people, among them 128 Americans, lost their lives. U.S. citizens were outraged, and

President Wilson declared he could not guarantee U.S. neutrality if the Germans continued submarine warfare against unarmed ships.

Wilson tried to keep the country out of the war, and many Americans agreed there should be no intervention. Some believed that those who supported U.S. involvement would gain financially from the war, while others objected to military action on moral and religious grounds.

One group of women led by Jane Addams, who founded Chicago's Hull House to assist the city's poorest residents, formed a Woman's Peace Party (WPP). Representatives of WPP traveled to The Hague in the Netherlands to participate in an international meeting of women to focus on peace.

In Mother Jones's opinion, "women with a consciousness of what war means to the children yet to come" could stop the war in Europe. Let the European men, "all grown fellows," fight each other if that's what they wanted to do, she declared in one of her speeches, but "let us fight at home to preserve this country."

By 1916, the Germans appeared ready to negotiate for peace, but they were really stalling for time and soon began again to attack neutral ships they thought were supplying the British. In March 1917, U-boats sank several American cargo ships, and President Wilson could no longer ignore the violations of U.S. neutrality. He went to Congress and asked for a declaration of war, which was granted on April 6, 1917. In his address to

President Woodrow Wilson appears before Congress in 1917 to ask for a declaration of war. (Library of Congress)

Congress, Wilson said that U.S. involvement would help keep the world "safe for democracy."

As the United States prepared for war, Americans were divided. The majority supported the war efforts, but Socialists, peace activists, and other dissenters were steadfastly opposed to armed conflict. Although Mother Jones had Socialist ideals, she and most other labor organizers changed their positions once the United States declared war on Germany. Speaking to union members in 1918, she explained, "If we are going to have freedom for the workers, we have got to stand behind the nation to the last man. . . . Perhaps I was as much opposed to war as anyone in the nation, but when we get into a fight I am one of those who intend to clean hell out of the other fellow, and we have got to clean the kaiser up," she said, referring to German Kaiser Wilhelm. She went on, "Now, mind you, I don't mean the German people; I mean the kaiser, the dictator; I mean the grafter, the burglar, the thief, the murderer."

The UMW and other national unions lined up behind the war effort. Samuel Gompers, head of the American Federation of Labor, became a member of the Council on National Defense, which helped create federal agencies to regulate labor and industry relations. He also asked unions not to strike during the war.

However, there were strikes—thousands of them—between 1917 and 1918. Women laundry workers in Kansas City started a strike in 1918 that influenced streetcar workers who were members of the Amalgamated Association of Streetcar and Electric Railwaymen. Streetcars were the primary means of transit, and when the laundry and streetcar workers united in a general strike, they successfully shut down the city for almost a week and gained some benefits in the process.

During the war, the federal government took control of major industries, regulating what they could buy and produce and where they could locate factories. A federal council set up a food-control program. Sugar and coal rationing began, and government agencies spread propaganda across the country, telling people what was or was not patriotic behavior. The post office even banned publications that carried antiwar articles.

Another part of the federal government's propaganda campaign was to portray Germans as evil and barbarous. German music and language courses were banned, while a popular German food, sauerkraut, was given a new label: liberty cabbage. Anti-German mania even tarred loyal German-Americans, many of whom were persecuted just because of their ancestry. It did not help that numerous German-Americans were Socialists and peace activists. The Socialist Party, a longtime supporter of the working class, was against the war and declared it would oppose the war "through demonstrations, mass petitions, and all other means within our power."

Socialist leader Eugene Debs was in the forefront of antiwar efforts. He delivered speeches that castigated the "master class" for advocating a war that the "subject class" had to fight. In one speech he noted, "The master class has had all to gain and nothing to lose, while the subject class has had nothing to gain and all to lose— including their lives . . . the working class who freely shed their blood and furnish the corpses, have never yet had a voice in declaring war or making peace. It is the ruling class that invariably does both."

Because of his antiwar activities, Debs was arrested and imprisoned for violating two federal laws: the Espionage Act of 1917 and the Sedition Act of 1918. Both were designed to prevent opposition to U.S. war efforts and provided heavy penalties for those who refused to do military service, obstructed the draft, or urged resistance to federal laws.

Under the acts, not only Socialists but also hundreds of conscientious objectors—those who object to war on a religious, moral, or ethical basis—and other antiwar citizens were arrested and imprisoned. Prisoners were subjected to brutal treatment and torture. Many foreign-born laborers and anarchists were deported. Especially hard hit were members of the Industrial Workers of the World, the radical labor union that Debs and Mother Jones helped establish. Dozens of leaders were arrested, tried, and sentenced to prison. The union was fined $2.5 million, which broke the IWW.

Although Mother Jones had previously supported Eugene Debs, the Socialist Party, and the IWW, she did not agitate on their behalf during the war. Instead, she made it clear that she expected workers to get behind the war effort and President Wilson, who was, she said, the first president to recognize labor. She urged UMW members to dig the coal and, if they had difficulties, "go to the national government and put our case before them before any strike is called. . . . Show the world there is one grand body of men in America that stands loyally for the flag. . . . Every star in that flag was bought with the blood of men who believed in freedom, industrial freedom, particularly. Now it is up to us to carry on the work. Organize, organize, organize." And organize is exactly what workers did.

8.
Down But
Not Out

During the war, the federal government encouraged industries to cooperate with labor unions and to provide wage increases and shorter workdays for employees. As Mother Jones put it, "working people were made to believe they amounted to something. . . . Up and down the land workers heard the word 'democracy.' . . . They were told that their labor, their money, their flesh were the bulwarks against tyranny and autocracy."

After the armistice of November 1918 and the end of the war, however, American industry was not as inclined to cooperate with labor. Furthermore, prices for most necessities were increasing, and workers feared they would lose the benefits they had won. In 1919, millions of workers went out on strike for pay raises. Strikers included cigar makers, carpenters, barbers, textile workers, city workers, and policemen.

One strike, in February, involved tens of thousands of workers in Seattle, Washington. It was the nation's largest general strike and an example of the union solidarity that the IWW had advocated for years. The strike began with Puget Sound shipyard workers, who wanted a pay raise to compensate for two years of wartime wage controls the federal government had imposed. Federal regulators refused to increase wages, and the U.S. government, working with the employers, ordered shipyard workers locked out of their jobs. To Seattle workers the lockout was just one more attempt to eliminate the gains they had made during the war.

That month, an alliance of AFL shipyard union members and more than one hundred other AFL unions, some IWW members, and nonunion workers were on strike. Ships stayed in port, businesses closed, most newspapers stopped publishing, streetcars could not run, and people feared shortages of food and fuel.

The peaceful strike ended in five days, primarily because the shut-down city was adversely affecting strikers as well as the rest of the population. But government officials—both state and federal—were convinced that the "Seattle strike was an attempted revolution," as the mayor of the city declared. He claimed the intent of the strike "was for the overthrow of the industrial system." That attitude persisted across the country, prompted by working-class rebellions not only in the United States but also in other nations such as Italy, Great Britain, and Germany.

In Russia, which became the Union of the Soviet Socialist Republics (USSR), the Bolshevik party (Communists) had dethroned the czar and established a Socialist state in 1917. Fear spread that Communists would overthrow other governments. From 1918 to 1921, Americans were obsessed with the threat of Communists, called Reds because of the red flag carried by Socialist and Communist groups as well as labor organizations. In the United States, however, Socialists were more intent on taking away the power of corporations and gaining public control of industries than in having an armed revolution. Still, the Red Scare intensified with the many strikes of 1919. One that involved hundreds of thousands of workers occurred at the steel mills in Pennsylvania.

For years after the 1892 strike at the Carnegie steel mills in Homestead, Pennsylvania, union activity was stifled; the company vowed never again to allow labor to organize. By 1900, Carnegie Steel had merged with the United States Steel Corporation, which operated mills in ten states, and official opposition to unions continued.

In 1918, the American Federation of Labor set up a national committee to organize steel workers, whose twelve-hour work day, seven days a week in intense heat, was exhausting, debilitating, and extremely dangerous. Steel towns were similar to coal towns—company-owned and tightly controlled by company guards.

While providing convenient and ready accommodations for workers in Pittsburgh, company-owned housing further indebted employees to the steel companies that controlled much of the city. (Library of Congress)

The AFL National Organizing Committee brought together representatives of two dozen craft unions, from blacksmiths to smelters to tin workers. Organizing the varied unions was difficult, not only because of the diversity of trades and scattered locations but also because workers, most of whom were immigrants, spoke various languages and sometimes little or no English. That was one of the reasons U.S. Steel hired the immigrants, and the company even gave the impression that it was part of the U.S. government, another way to intimidate foreign workers.

Judge Elbert Gary, president of U.S. Steel, authorized many tactics to prevent workers from organizing. One ploy was to get the courts to order injunctions that banned any union meetings. Another was to send guards to break up gatherings by force. Still, unionization went slowly forward.

Few steelworkers were union members in western Pennsylvania, so in August 1919, the UMW sent Mother Jones to Pittsburgh to help AFL committee leaders John Fitzpatrick—Jones's friend and president of the Chicago Federation of Labor—and former IWW member William Foster to organize. Jones, now quite elderly, led protest marches and gave numerous speeches. She addressed more than 3,000 iron and steel workers at a Pittsburgh hall that became the headquarters for the AFL Organizing Committee.

At another gathering she spoke to workers assembled in the street. Police arrested her and three other organizers for not having a permit to hold a meeting. A crowd gathered outside the jail and began demanding Mother Jones's release. Her jailer asked her to speak to the men, which she did, assuring them that she would be released soon on bail. She convinced the men to leave peacefully.

The next day Jones and the other organizers appeared in a Pittsburgh court, where Jones claimed that she had a permit to speak on the street. The judge asked her who issued the permit, and Jones replied, "Patrick Henry, Thomas Jefferson, and John Adams." She and the others were released after paying a heavy fine. Jones used this story numerous times to remind her audiences that

U.S. Steel Corporation President Judge Elbert Gary. (Northwestern University Archives)

American forefathers had been instrumental in obtaining citizens the rights to free speech and freedom of assembly.

Although AFL President Gompers tried to negotiate with U.S. Steel, Elbert Gary refused to meet. Even President Wilson could not persuade Gary to meet with union representatives. As a result, the AFL Committee distributed a strike ballot to workers. Because of the varied nationalities of the workers, the ballot was printed in English, Croatian, Hungarian, Italian, Polish, and Slovak. The vote was an overwhelming "Yes," and on September 22, workers walked out in steel towns such as Gary, Indiana; Cleveland and Youngstown, Ohio; Pittsburgh,

Pennsylvania; Wheeling, West Virginia, and others. Anywhere from 250,000 to more than 300,000 workers promised to stay out until their demands were met. These demands included a pay increase, an eight-hour work day, a six-day week, and the right to be represented by their own union, not the company organization patterned after the Rockefeller plan.

During the strike, Mother Jones traveled by rail to mill towns in Pennsylvania, Ohio, Indiana, and Illinois to talk to strikers and their families. She often risked imprisonment—and indeed was jailed several times—for what officials called unlawful assembly. Local police, state militia, and federal troops were constantly a presence, ready to brutalize, arrest, and imprison strikers. Steel company owners used every possible means to discourage and prevent workers from organizing.

The general public and news organizations had little sympathy for unions or Mother Jones. Many Americans believed that union organizers and strikers were Bolsheviks, the Russian Communists, stirring up a revolution, a charge often made by officials in the U.S. Department of Justice and other government agencies.

When Mother Jones was in Gary, Indiana, on October 23, 1919, to speak to strikers, she used the Bolshevik accusation to lambaste the owners of the steel works and their supporters, "the damned gang of robbers and political thieves" who, she declared, would "start the American revolution." She said, "I'll be 90 years old the first of May, but by God I'll take

90 guns and shoot the hell out of them if I have to."

The hall where Jones spoke to 1,200 strikers and their wives was guarded inside and out by federal troops. At one point she told the soldiers, "You went abroad to clean up the Kaiser, and the bones of 60,000 of your buddies lie bleaching on the battlefields of France. My God, ain't you men enough to come over and help us get the Kaisers at home?" She dared them to arrest her, saying she would still "be free. I can raise more hell in jail than out. If Bolshevist is what I understand it to be, then I'm a Bolshevist from the bottom of my feet to the top of my head."

Her statement did not help the cause. The Red Scare was real to many Americans, and support for unionization was not forthcoming. Steel corporations brought in large numbers of temporary workers to keep the mills going. Companies also hired a strikebreaking service to pit one group of strikers against another, telling strikebreakers, "We want you to stir up as much bad feeling as you possibly can between the Serbians and Italians. Spread data among the Serbians that the Italians are going back to work." Serbians were urged to return to the mills before the Italians could get their jobs. After six weeks, the strike began to weaken as men slowly went back to the mills. By January 8, 1920, it was over.

Mother Jones certainly experienced, along with the strikers, that terrible defeat. She wrote:

The strike was broken. Broken by the scabs brought

in under the protection of the troops. Broken by
breaking men's belief in the outcome of their
struggle. Broken by breaking men's hearts. Broken
by the press, the government.... At the headquarters
men wept. I wept with them.

After the strike, Jones, who was suffering from rheumatism, went to California for a brief rest, staying with
wealthy union supporters. But the nation was not at rest
in 1920, or for that matter throughout the decade. Movies,
books, and plays have depicted the time as the Roaring
Twenties, with boundless wealth and unbridled enter-
tainment, but most working people in the United States
did not share in the prosperity. There was still much
unemployment, industries reduced wages, and union
membership fell.

One issue that had been under contention for years—
women's suffrage—finally came to a successful conclu-
sion with the adoption of the Nineteenth Amendment to
the U.S. Constitution, which granted women the right to
vote. According to some historians, women's suffrage
was an issue that Mother Jones opposed. Jones once
commented, "You don't need the vote to raise hell." She
also clearly stated that she was not a suffragist and
believed in human rights rather than women's or men's
rights. However, she declared in speeches that if women
were elected to office, they would find ways to improve
society. She expressed her indignation that women who
had won the right to vote had "never raised their voice"
to protest company thugs who shot and killed miners.

"What good is the ballot if [women] don't use it?" she asked in one speech. She also urged women to fight the ruling class that assaulted and destroyed women and children along with men. To Jones, this was the greater outrage, the issue that occupied most of her days and roused her passion.

Critics of Mother Jones found fault with her views on another issue of the 1920s: alcohol prohibition. The Eighteenth Amendment to the U.S. Constitution (ratified in 1919) went into effect on January 16, 1920, and prohibited the import, export, transport, sale, and manu-facture of intoxicating liquors. Jones had no use for the ban, calling it "a national farce" that had been brought

In 1923, prohibition agents raid a working-class lunchroom in Washington, DC, during the height of enforcement of the government's ban on alcohol. (Library of Congress)

about by "a lot of preachers and a group of damn cats who threw fits when they saw a workingman buy a bottle of beer but saw no reason to bristle when [workers and their families] suffered under the curse of low wages and crushing hours of toil." Saloons, she noted, were the workers' only social clubs and were closed down, but the rich "have their clubs which are sacred and immune from interference."

On that point, she was right. Prominent citizens and politicians could easily buy illegal alcoholic drinks at private clubs and in secret back rooms of businesses. Prohibition was supposed to reduce social problems and crime and create a healthier society. But even though alcohol consumption dropped for a short time, illegal brewing and bootlegging—selling and distributing— went on, and drinking increased. Prohibition laws were only loosely enforced, and most of the financial benefits ended up in the pockets of gangsters who controlled the bootlegging activities. Prohibition failed, and Congress repealed the Eighteenth Amendment in 1933, several years after Mother Jones's death.

Jones sometimes mentioned in her speeches during the 1920s that her days were numbered. Her health was failing, and she traveled less frequently. On occasion she had to stay with friends or go to the hospital to relieve rheumatic pain or other illness. But she still managed to deliver speeches and grant interviews. She also kept in-formed about the labor movement and the anti-immigrant sentiments that were widespread in the United States.

Continued unrest and negative public opinion of Socialists and Communists contributed to a significant decline of labor unions in the 1920s—from 5.1 million union members in 1920 to fewer than 3.5 million members in 1929. Early in the decade, many workers lost their jobs because companies needed fewer employees. New methods of mass production forced workers to speed up their tasks and produce more than they had -previously. In addition, some companies moved their locations from traditional union strongholds to places where trade unions had not been formed. Another tactic to stop unionizing was a demand that workers sign agreements, called yellow-dog contracts, not to join a union.

Legislators also played a role in union decline. In a letter to Mother Jones, John Walker, president of the Illinois Federation of Labor, noted "We are having a desperate battle here. There are four bills in [the legislature] that the enemies of labor are pushing strongly. Either one of them if enacted into law will do away with the present form of trade unions in our state." Mother Jones's reply was as gloomy: "Things do not look very bright to me . . . everywhere they are passing bills to crush labor."

Jones was also experiencing her own crushing blows—advancing age, physical deterioration, and a lack of funds. But always feisty, she did not stop her traveling and speaking altogether. She went to Mexico twice in 1921 to help unify workers there and to support the Pan-American Federation of Labor. When she returned to the United States, she stayed for a time at John Walker's home in Springfield, Illinois, so that she could consult with a specialist about her rheumatism. "I am suffering severely, and unable to do anything outside of moaning about my troubles," she wrote to Terence Powderly, faithful friend and former head of the Knights of Labor.

When she recovered enough to travel, she left Springfield and went to Washington, DC, to stay with the Powderlys, who considered her one of the family and always kept a spare bedroom ready for her visits. Powderly himself was in poor health, but he paid for much of

Mother Jones in the 1920s. (Library of Congress)

Jones's medical care as well as other expenses. While with the Powderlys, other friends—Walter Burgess, a retired miner, and his wife, Lillie Mae—visited and took Jones for rides to their farm in Maryland.

Within a few weeks, Jones was in better health and able to take a trip to Chicago. There she met with magazine writer Molly Field Parton, who had agreed to help Jones with her autobiography, taking dictation and transcribing Jones's words. But Mother Jones soon tired of the project, and some historians speculate that her fatigue, advanced age, and illness contributed to some of the inaccuracies and jumbled chronology in her completed book, published in 1925. Before its publication, however, Jones still had some agitating she wanted to do.

9.
Last Years

T hough Mary Jones was as wary of politicians as she was other authority figures, there was a political fight going on that she could not ignore. Discouraged by a lack of attention from the Republican and Democratic parties, a coalition of farmers and laborers in the Midwest joined together to form a third political party. Farmers hoped to obtain better prices for their crops, while laborers wanted better wages and a shorter workweek.

Jones supported the Farmer-Labor Party and traveled to Chicago to speak at a convention in 1923. She also encouraged delegates from the Workers' Party and the Communist Party, who developed a platform calling for an eight-hour workday, a ban on child labor, and for farmers and workers to have control over industry.

However, other delegates objected to the Communist influence at the convention and walked out to form their own political party, the Federated Farmer-Labor Party.

Speaking at the convention, Jones took aim at the established political parties, as well as "crooked labor leaders" who betrayed workers by taking jobs with the very companies that oppressed labor. Mother Jones also was aware of instances of outright corruption by labor leaders who stole union funds to use for their own purposes or rigged union elections to stay in power.

Neither third-party faction survived, dying out within a year. Mother Jones was disheartened by the lack of unity in the third-party movement, but she continued to speak out and write about her dream for a Socialist state and her admiration for the accomplishments in Soviet Russia. In reality, however, Russia's attempt at creating a Socialist state would be a dismal failure and take the lives of millions of its citizens. But the truth about Joseph Stalin's murderous regime was only slowly emerging. Meanwhile, many Socialists in America held out hope that Russia's experiment would prove to be a success. Jones wrote hopefully in her autobiography that Soviet Russia "had dared to challenge the old order, had handed the earth over to those who toiled upon it, and the capitalists of the world were quaking in their scab-made shoes."

There were few capitalists or major industrialists "quaking" in the United States, however. Instead, with government and police support, they were able to suppress strikes wherever they took place. In February

1924, for example, 3,000 dressmakers—90 percent of them women—walked out in a strike against dress manufacturers in Chicago. Mother Jones was there urging the strikers on. Once more though, a judge ordered an injunction against strikers, and hundreds of women were attacked by police and arrested for violating the injunction, effectively ending the strike in July.

A month before the strike was defeated, Mother Jones's friend Terence Powderly died, and Jones returned to Washington, DC. After the funeral, she traveled to Southern California, where she sought pardons for labor organizers imprisoned in the state penitentiary.

A ceaseless mouthpiece for the American worker, an aging Mother Jones speaks with President Calvin Coolidge in September 1924. (Library of Congress)

Her pleas to governors on behalf of jailed union members were not always successful, but she continued her efforts during her declining years. When her autobiography was published in 1925, she hoped to use income from the book to set up a defense fund for jailed workers. But the book did not sell well, in spite of the glowing introduction by the famed attorney Clarence Darrow. He described Mother Jones as "essentially an individualist . . . always doubtful of the good of organized institutions. These require compromises and she could not compromise." Darrow noted:

> This little book is a story of a woman of action fired by a fine zeal. She defied calumny. She was not awed by guns or jails. She kept on her way regardless of friends and foes. She had but one love to which she was always true and that was her cause.

The "little book" was almost forgotten in the years following its original publication, although it was reissued in the 1970s. Jones did little to promote her autobiography, claiming she did not like it. But the truth was she was in poor health.

As her health continued to fail, Mother Jones depended on Emma Powderly to care for her, until the efforts became too much for the aged Emma. In 1928, Mother Jones went to live with Walter and Lillie Mae Burgess. Most of the time she was bedridden. Nevertheless, she had many visitors and frequently talked with them about the labor movement. She also made plans for her one hundredth birthday party, to be celebrated on May 1, 1930, her chosen birth date.

Historians speculate that Mother Jones chose that birth date during her early activist years because it was the International Workers' Day, established in 1886 in the United States to mark labor's fight for an eight-hour work day. Today, working people worldwide celebrate the achievements of workers on May 1, but the date is not recognized in the United States because of its Socialist and Communist ties. Instead, Labor Day is celebrated on the first Monday in September.

On May 1, 1930, Mother Jones did indeed have her birthday party, despite pneumonia that had weakened her and kept her in bed for months. The celebration was held on the lawn of the Burgess family home. Jones sat in a rocker and greeted hundreds of people. The festive affair included a cake with one hundred candles, dozens of other cakes, tubs of punch, sandwiches, bunting, flowers, a band, and congratulatory telegrams.

Reporters were there with a newsreel camera to cover the event. Before the camera rolled, the photographer tried to tell Mother Jones what to say, but in no uncertain terms, she informed him that she had been making speeches before he was born. When she turned to the camera, she delivered her last speech, saying in part,

> Power lies in the hands of labor to retain American liberty, but labor has not yet learned how to use that

power. A wonderful power is in the hands of women, too, but they don't know how to use it. Capitalists sidetrack the women into clubs and make ladies of them. Nobody wants a lady, they want women. Ladies are parlor parasites.

After her birthday party, Mother Jones made no further public appearances. Over the next six months she slowly faded away. She died November 30, 1930, at the Burgess home.

Mother Jones poses with a five-tiered cake in celebration of her one hundredth birthday on May 1, 1930. (Courtesy of Getty Images.)

For two years after Mother Jones's death, hundreds of people traveled to the Burgess farm to pay their respects at a shrine set up in her former room. Lillie Mae later turned her home at Powder Mill and Riggs Road in Adelphi, Prince Georges County, Maryland, into the Mother Jones Rest Home. It has since been torn down, but in 2000, the state of Maryland placed a historical marker on the site where Jones died. A school in Adelphi is also named for her: Mary Harris "Mother" Jones Elementary.

The funeral for Mother Jones was held not far from the Burgess home at St. Gabriel's Roman Catholic Church in Washington, DC. Union officials, some government dignitaries, working people and their families, and even a group of unemployed men attended. A railcar carried her remains to Mt. Olive, Illinois, where 20,000 to 30,000 people assembled for the burial of Jones's body alongside her "boys."

Over a six-year period, union miners raised funds for a memorial at the burial site, and they donated their labor to erect a granite obelisk with a great medallion bearing the likeness of Mother Jones. On either side of the obelisk stands a larger-than-life bronze statue of a coal miner with his sledge. At the base, the engraving reads the way Mother Jones intended:

Mary "Mother" Jones
Born May 1, 1830
Died November 30, 1930

A simple stone marks the grave with her name.

At the dedication of the monument in 1936, an estimated 50,000 people came by five special trains, twenty-five buses, and private cars. Some even hitchhiked to the site to pay homage to Mother Jones and her five decades of activism.

Contemporaries who knew her expected that she would be long remembered. Over the years, though, the general public lost interest in the agitator for the labor movement, until the 1970s when new editions of her autobiography and the first book about her life were published. In the decades that followed, several other historians published their accounts of Mother Jones.

Arguably, one of today's most important reminders of Mother Jones and her legacy is the magazine named for her. *Mother Jones* began publication in 1976 and is committed to social justice and independent investigative reporting. In its twenty-fifth anniversary issue, the magazine editors noted that the "founders envisioned a magazine devoted to a new brand of socially conscious journalism—one that took on corporate as well as political power." These are the very same crusades that working people fought (and are still fighting today), crusades that Mary Harris "Mother" Jones championed most of her adult life.

In the early 1900s, Joe Hill, an immigrant from Sweden, drifted from job to job, writing songs and poems. When he joined the International Workers of the World in 1910, he began writing songs about labor issues. Four years later he was unjustly convicted of a murder and, in spite of wide public protest, he was executed in 1915. The night before he faced the firing squad, he wrote to IWW leader William "Big Bill" Haywood telling him, "Don't waste any time in mourning, organize!" Those words became a motto for the IWW.

Although Mother Jones was one of the founders of the IWW, she distanced herself from the organization because of its lack of unity and infighting. She also disagreed with some of its positions, which she considered more radical than her own. Whatever her views about the IWW, Mother Jones on occasion expressed some of the same sentiments that Joe Hill wrote about in one of his songs:

Workers of the world awaken!
Break your chains, demand your rights.
All the wealth you make is taken,
by exploiting parasites.
Shall you kneel in deep submission
from your cradle to your grave.
Is the height of your ambition
to be a good and willing slave?

TIMELINE

1837	Mary Harris born (exact date unknown) in Cork County, Ireland.
1847	(Approximately) Harris's father and older brother sail from Ireland to North America.
1849	Mary and the rest of her family emigrate to Canada.
1959	Harris becomes a secular teacher in a Catholic school in Michigan.
1860	Moves to Chicago, sets up dressmaking shop; moves again to Memphis, Tennessee, and meets George Jones.
1861	Mary Harris and George Jones marry.
1867	Yellow fever epidemic kills all four of the Jones children and George Jones; Mary moves to Chicago.
1871	Great Chicago Fire destroys Mary Jones's dressmaking business and home.
1891	Organizes miners for newly formed United Mine Workers of America.
1894	Raises funds for "Coxey's Army"; organizes miners and investigates cotton mills in the South.
1896	Helps launch *Appeal to Reason*, a Socialist weekly.
1897	After massacre of strikers in Lattimer, Pennsylvania, works with UMW to organize nationwide strike of bituminous (soft) coal miners.
1901-1902	Organizes miners in Pennsylvania, Virginia, and West Virginia.

1903	Leads a march of children from Pennsylvania to President Roosevelt's home in New York; goes to Colorado to organize miners.
1904	Resigns her position as international organizer with the UMW.
1905	Helps found the Industrial Workers of the World (IWW).
1907-1910	Campaigns for Mexican liberation and raises defense funds for jailed Mexican rebels.
1912-1913	Works with striking miners in West Virginia; tried and convicted in West Virginia militia court for conspiracy to commit murder and sentenced to twenty years; U.S. Senate investigates her imprisonment, and she is freed.
1913-1914	Returns to Colorado to aid in miners' strikes; deported from the state and returns again; imprisoned several times; after Ludlow Massacre, travels to publicize the killing of women and children in strikers' tent colony.
1915-1916	Travels extensively and works with Western Federation of Miners; helps streetcar, garment, and steel workers organize; speaks and writes on behalf of framed union organizers serving prison sentences.
1917	Reverses her antiwar stance and supports U.S. entry in World War I.
1919	Aids workers in steel strike; gets arrested several times.
1920	Criticizes alcohol prohibition.
1921	Addresses the Pan American Federation of Labor in Mexico City.
1923	Speaks to Farmer-Labor Party in Chicago.
1924	Writes autobiography (with help of Mary Field Parton); lives with Terence and Emma Powderly; Terence dies.
1930	Celebrates supposed one hundredth birthday (actually her ninety-second); dies November 30.

SOURCES

CHAPTER ONE: Born to Agitate

p. 9-10, "This great gathering that is . . ." Timothy Patrick McCarthy and John McMillan eds., *The Radical Reader: A Documentary History of the American Radical Tradition* (New York & London: The New Press, 2003), 296-297.

p. 11, "In all the great . . ." Mary Harris Jones, *Autobiography of Mother Jones*, ed. Mary Field Parton (Mineola, NY: Dover Publications, 2004), 5.

p. 12, "I was born in the city . . ." Ibid., 1.

p. 15, "Disease and death . . ." "Skibbereen," *The Cork Examiner,* November 27, 1846, http://vassun.vassar.edu/~sttaylor/FAMINE/Examiner/Archives/Nov1846.html (accessed January 2006).

p. 15-16, "crowded beyond its . . ." Howard Zinn, *A People's History of the United States* (New York: Perennial Classics/HarperCollins, 2003), 226.

p. 17, "but always as the child . . ." Jones, *Autobiography of Mother Jones*, 1.

p. 17, "a good brand of popular . . . truth about conditions," Philip S. Foner, ed., *Mother Jones Speaks,* 4th ed. (New York: Pathfinder, 2001), 650.

p. 18, "Miss M. Harris entered . . . $36.43," Judith Nies, *Nine Women: Portraits from the American Radical Tradition* (Berkeley: University of California Press, 2002), 98.

CHAPTER TWO: Marriage, Children, and Tragedy

p. 19, "bossing little children," Jones, *Autobiography of Mother Jones,* 1.

p. 21, "the other civil war," Zinn, *A People's History of the United States,* 211.

p. 25, "Across the street from me . . ." Jones, *Autobiography of Mother Jones,* 1-2.

p. 25, "Pray for the dead . . ." Ibid., 21.

p. 26, "aristocrats . . . nor to care," Ibid., 2.

CHAPTER THREE: Becoming an Activist

p. 31, "splendid speakers," Jones, *Autobiography of Mother Jones*, 2.

p. 31, "more and more engrossed . . ." Ibid., 3.

p. 32, "she was out of place . . ." Nies, *Nine Women,* 102.

p. 32, "bread for the needy . . ." Zinn, *A People's History of the United States*, 243.

p. 33, "knew the strikers personally," Jones, *Autobiography of Mother Jones*, 3.

p. 34-35, "Steadily they approached . . ." McCarthy, *The Radical Reader,* 240-241.

p. 35, "the feeling at . . . to keep order," Foner, *Mother Jones Speaks,* 518.

p. 36, "The workers asked . . ." Jones, *Autobiography of Mother Jones,* 5.

p. 37, "made the government . . ." Edward M. Steel, ed., *The Speeches and Writings of Mother Jones* (Pittsburgh, PA: University of Pittsburgh Press, 1988), 251-252.

p. 39, "I never endorsed . . ." Jones, *Autobiography of Mother Jones*, 6.

p. 39-40, "in rags and tatters . . ." Ibid., 6-7.

p. 41, "The city went insane . . ." Ibid., 7-8.

p. 41, "convict these men . . ." Philip S. Foner, ed., *The Autobiographies of the Haymarket Martyrs* (New York: Humanities Press, 1969), 8.

p. 42, "outwitted the gallows . . . workers' struggle," Jones, *Autobiography of Mother Jones*, 8.

p. 42, "police not only . . ." John P. Altgeld, *Altgeld's Pardon Message* (Chicago: Charles H. Kerr Publishing, 1986), 36.

CHAPTER FOUR: Organizing Workers

p. 54, "When we got down . . ." Jones, *Autobiography of Mother Jones*, 69.

p. 54-55, "the aisles, the window . . ." Ibid.

p. 55, "a drink with the boys . . ." John Brophy, *A Miner's Life* (Madison: University of Wisconsin Press, 1964), 74.

p. 56, "bucked and kicked . . . did not bring in scabs," Jones, *Autobiography of Mother Jones*, 17.

p. 57, "it is solidarity of labor . . ." Ibid., 17.

CHAPTER FIVE: Theatrics and Politics

p. 63, "most dangerous woman . . ." Jones, *Autobiography of Mother Jones*, 27.

p. 63, "Well, I can't call him . . ." Ibid., 27-28.

p. 63, "be a good girl . . ." Steel, *The Speeches and Writings of Mother Jones*, 18.

p. 63, "I asked my lawyer . . ." Ibid.

p. 63, "reckless agitators . . . to pursue," Dale Fetherling, *Mother Jones the Miners' Angel: A Portrait* (Carbondale: Southern Illinois University Press, 1974), 33.

p. 66, "Vigorously I stoked . . ." Richard B. Morris and James Woodress, eds., *Voices from America's Past: 2* (New York: E. P. Dutton, 1963), 196.

p. 66-67, "dragged out of bed . . . thrown out to die," Steel, *The Speeches and Writings of Mother Jones*, 265.

p. 68, "torture and murder . . .cruelty" Ibid., 267.

p. 68, "was burdened with . . ." Jones, *Autobiography of Mother Jones*, 74.

p. 68, "Philadelphia's mansions . . ." Ibid., 40-41.

p. 72-73, "began her speech . . ." Foner, *Mother Jones Speaks*, 46.

p. 73, "created practical peonage . . ." Jones, *Autobiography of Mother Jones*, 58.

p. 73, "with eighteen inches . . ." Ibid.

p. 73, "the guns were turned on me . . ." Ibid.

p. 75, "confederate the workers . . ." Melvyn Dubofsy, *We Shall Be All: A History of the Industrial Workers of the World* (New York: Quadrangle Books, 1969), 81.

p. 75, "The working class and . . ." Kathlyn Gay and Martin Gay, *Encyclopedia of Political Anarchy* (Santa Barbara, CA: ABC-Clio, 1999), 107.

p. 77, "church bell tolls . . ." Elliott J. Gorn, *Mother Jones: The Most Dangerous Woman in America* (New York: Hill and Wang, 2001), 147.

CHAPTER SIX: Imprisoned

p. 79, "We have got to get . . . off their bodies," Steel, *The Speeches and Writings of Mother Jones*, 28-29.

p. 80, "My address is . . ." Jones, *Autobiography of Mother Jones*, 82.

p. 80, "Gentlemen, in the . . ." Ibid., 85.

p. 80-81, "Brothers and Comrades . . . they may be shot," Steel, *The Speeches and Writings of Mother Jones,* 285.

p. 82-83, "I am a working girl . . ." Eleanor Flexner, *Century of Struggle: The Woman's Rights Movement in the United States* (New York: Atheneum, 1974), 241.

p. 83-84, "This is not a play . . . they will be afraid of you!" Foner, *Mother Jones Speaks,* 172.

p. 84, "for the time when . . ." Ibid., 173.

p. 85, "The miners had . . ." Jones, *Autobiography of Mother Jones*, 89.

p. 86, "that was the only . . ." Ibid., 94.

p. 86-87, "If you shoot . . . jack rabbits, perhaps," Ibid., 95.

p. 90, "Rise up and strike! . . ." Fetherling, *Mother Jones the Miners' Angel*, 114.

p. 91, "It was a cold . . ." Jones, *Autobiography of Mother Jones*, 112.

p. 93, "If the men of . . ." Gorn, *Mother Jones: The Most Dangerous Woman in America*, 211.

CHAPTER SEVEN: More Battles

p. 96, "No time in modern . . ." Steel, *The Speeches and Writings of Mother Jones*, 131.

p. 98, "The sword will have to . . ." Ibid., 151.

p. 98, "the other side had . . ." Jones, *Autobiography of Mother Jones*, 124.

p. 99, "Capital cannot move . . ." Henry P. Guzda, "Industrial Democracy: Made in The U.S.A.," *Monthly Labor Review*, May 1984, 28.

p. 100, "a sham and fraud," Jones, *Autobiography of Mother Jones*, 124.

p. 100, "There is no doubt . . ." Steel, *The Speeches and Writings of Mother Jones,* 161-162.

p. 101, "The old farmer said . . ." Ibid., 166.

p. 102, "Thank God I have . . ." Foner, *Mother Jones Speaks*, 352.

p. 103, "women with . . . preserve this country," Steel, *The Speeches and Writings of Mother Jones*, 178-179.

p. 104, "safe for democracy," Arthur S. Link, *Woodrow Wilson: A Brief Biography* (Cleveland, OH: The World Publishing Company, 1963), 113.

p. 104-105, "If we are . . . the thief, the murderer," Foner, *Mother Jones Speaks*, 371-372.

p. 106, "through demonstrations . . ." Ibid., 373.

p. 106, "The master class . . ." Eugene Debs, *Writings and Speeches of Eugene V. Debs* (New York: Hermitage Press, 1948), 425.

p. 107, "go to the . . ." Foner, *Mother Jones Speaks,* 379-380.

CHAPTER EIGHT: Down But Not Out

p. 108, "working people were . . ." Jones, *Autobiography of Mother Jones*, 129.

p. 109, "Seattle strike was . . ." Zinn, *A People's History of the United States*, 379.

p. 112, "Patrick Henry, Thomas Jefferson . . ." Jones, *Autobiography of Mother Jones*, 131.

p. 114-115, "the damned gang . . ." Foner, *Mother Jones Speaks*, 406.

p. 115, "You went abroad . . . of my head," Ibid., 407.

p. 115, "We want you . . ." Zinn, *A People's History of the United States*, 381.

p. 115-116, "The strike was . . ." Jones, *Autobiography of Mother Jones*, 138.

p. 116, "You don't need . . ." Ibid.,125.

p. 116-117, "never raised . . . don't use it?" Foner, *Mother Jones Speaks*, 434.

p. 117-118, "a national farce . . . from interference," Jones, *Autobiography of Mother Jones*, 148.

p. 119, "We are having . . . crush labor," Foner, *Mother Jones Speaks*, 840-841.

p. 120, "I am suffering severely . . ." Ibid., 849.

CHAPTER NINE: Last Years

p. 123, "crooked labor leaders," Jones, *Autobiography of Mother Jones,* 147.

p. 123, "had dared to challenge . . ." Ibid., 148.

p. 125, "essentially . . . was her cause," Clarence Darrow in the introduction, *Autobiography of Mother Jones*, v-vi.

p. 126-127, "Power lies in the hands . . ." Ibid., 693.

p. 129, "founders envisioned a . . ." Adam Hochschild, *Mother Jones,* May/June 2001. http://www.motherjones.com/commentary/columns/2001/05/first25.html (accessed January 2006).

p. 130, "Don't waste any . . ." Joe Hill, "History: Joe Hill," AFL-CIO, http://www.aflcio.org/aboutus/history/history/hill.cfm (accessed January 2006).

p. 130, "Workers of the world . . ." Joe Hill, "Workers of the World, Awaken!" http://digital.library.arizona.edu/bisbee/docs/027.php (accessed January 2006).

BIBLIOGRAPHY

Altgeld, John P. *Altgeld's Pardon Message*. Chicago: Charles H. Kerr Publishing, 1986.

Atkinson, Linda. *Mother Jones, the Most Dangerous Woman in America*. New York: Crown Publishers, 1978.

Brophy, John. *A Miner's Life*. Madison: University of Wisconsin Press, 1964.

Debs, Eugene. *Writings and Speeches of Eugene V. Debs*. New York: Hermitage Press, 1948.

Dinon, Richard. *Rebel in Paradise: A Biography of Emma Goldman*. Chicago: University of Chicago Press, 1961.

Dubofsy, Melvyn. *We Shall Be All: A History of the Industrial Workers of the World*. New York: Quadrangle Books, 1969.

Fetherling, Dale. *Mother Jones the Miners' Angel*. Carbondale, IL: Southern Illinois University Press, 1974.

Flexner, Eleanor. *Century of Struggle: The Woman's Rights Movement in the United States*. New York: Atheneum, 1974.

Foner, Philip S., ed. *Mother Jones Speaks: Collected Writings and Speeches*. 4th ed. New York: Pathfinder, 2001.

———. The Autobiographies of the Haymarket Martyrs. New York: Humanities Press, 1969.

Gay, Kathlyn and Martin Gay. *Heroes of Conscience: A Biographical Dictionary*. Santa Barbara, CA: ABC-CLIO, 1996.

———. *Encyclopedia of Political Anarchy*. Santa Barbara, CA: ABC-Clio, 1999.

Gilbert, Ronnie. *Ronnie Gilbert on Mother Jones: Face to Face with the Most Dangerous Woman in America*. Berkeley, CA: Conari Press, 1993.

Gorn, Elliott. *Mother Jones: The Most Dangerous Woman in America* New York: Hill and Wang, 2001.

Guzda, Henry P. "Industrial Democracy: Made in The U.S.A." *Monthly Labor Review*. May 1984.

Hawxhurst, Joan C.. *Mother Jones: Labor Crusader*. Austin, TX: Steck-Vaughn, 1994.

Hill, Joe. "Workers of the World, Awaken!" http://digital. library.arizona.edu/bisbee/docs/027.php

Hochschild, Adam. *Mother Jones.* May/June 2001. http:// www.motherjones.com/commentary/columns/2001/05/ first25.html.

Jones, Mary Harris. *Autobiography of Mother Jones.* Mary Field Parton, ed.. Chicago: Charles H. Kerr & Co., 1925.

———. *Autobiography of Mother Jones.* New York: Arno, 1969.

Link, Arthur S. *Woodrow Wilson: A Brief Biography.* Cleveland, OH: The World Publishing Company, 1963.

McCarthy, Timothy Patrick and John McMillan, eds. *The Radical Reader: A Documentary History of the American Radical Tradition.* New York & London: The New Press, 2003.

Morris, Richard B. and James Woodress, eds. *Voices from America's Past: 2.* New York: E. P. Dutton, 1963.

Nies, Judith. *Nine Women: Portraits from the American Radical Tradition.* Berkeley and Los Angeles: University of California Press, 2002.

"Remission of Rents," *The Cork Examiner* December 18, 1846. http://vassun.vassar.edu/~sttaylor/FAMINE/Examiner/ Archives/Dec1846.html

Roberts, Ron E. and Carol Cook-Roberts. *Mother Jones and Her Sisters: A Century of Women Activists in the American Coal Fields.* Dubuque, Iowa: Kendall/Hunt, 1998.

"Skibbereen," *The Cork Examiner,* November 27, 1846. http:/ /vassun.vassar.edu/~sttaylor/FAMINE/Examiner/Archives/ Nov1846.html

Steel, Edward M., ed. *The Correspondence of Mother Jones.* Pittsburgh, PA: University of Pittsburgh Press, 1985.

———. *The Speeches and Writings of Mother Jones.* Pittsburgh, Pa.: University of Pittsburgh Press, 1988.

Wake, Dorothy L. *Mother Jones: Revolutionary Leader of Labor and Social Reform.* On-demand publisher, www.xlibris.com, 2001.

Werstein, Irving. *Labor's Defiant Lady.* New York: Thomas Crowell, Co., 1969.

Wexler, Alice. *Emma Goldman: An Intimate Life.* New York: Pantheon, 1984.

Zinn, Howard. *A People's History of the United States.* New York: Perennial Classics / HarperCollins, 2003.

WEB SITES

http://www.aflcio.org/aboutaflcio/history/history/jones.cfm
In 1955, the American Federation of Labor and the Congress of Industrial Organizations merged to form the AFL-CIO. Today, the union is nine million members strong.

http://www.iww.org/
The Industrial Workers of the World continue their efforts to overthrow the capitalist system, more than one hundred years after Mother Jones helped found this union.

http://www.umwa.org/history/mj1.shtml
The United Mine Workers of America Web site describes the goals and accomplishments of that still-active union, and offers a brief tribute to Mother Jones.

http://libraries.cua.edu/MotherJones/
In 1939, the papers of Terence Powderly were donated to Catholic University. In 1943, a set of letters between John Mitchell and Mother Jones was also donated to the university. This Web site offers the viewer scanned images of the actual letters and a selection of pictures.

http://www.pbs.org/newshour/bb/business/september96/labor_day_9-2.html
An article from PBS explains the origins and significance of Labor Day.

INDEX

58, 60, 72–74

National Child Labor Com-
mittee (NCLC), 70

Ogelsby, Richard, 42
O'Hare, Kate Richards, 61

Paint and Cabin Creek
Mines strike, 85–89, *86*
Parsons, Lucy, 61
Pay raise strikes of 1919,
108–109
Powderly, Terence, 46–47,
47, 120, 124
Progressives, 58-59, 61, 64
Prohibition, 117–118
Pullman, George, 51–53
Pullman Strike of 1894, 51–
53, *52*

Riis, Jacob, 59
Rockefeller, John D., 89,
100
Rockefeller Jr., John, 89,
93, 98–100, *99*
Roosevelt, Theodore, 58–60,
58, 69

Sarabia, Manuel, 78-80
Sinclair, Upton, 59
Socialism, 31, 55
Steel strike, 110–116

Tarbell, Ida, 59

United Mine Worker's of
America (UMW), 44, 54,
56, 57, 60, 70–74, 78,
79, 85, 89, 95, 96, 98,
105

Western Federation of
Miners (WFM), 71
Wilson, Woodrow, 93, 96–
98, 103, 104, *104*
Woman's Peace Party
(WPP), 103
Women suffrage, 116–117
Women's Trade Union
League (WTUL), 82
Workingmen's Party of
California, 36
World War I, 102–105

Yellow-fever epidemic, 23–
25, *24*